Practical Cinematography and Its Applications

Practical Cinematography

and its Applications

CALIFORNIA

Motograph Co.

How to take Moving-pictures of Wild Animals in Safety.

Messrs. Newman built a huge dummy cow fifteen feet in height of papier-mâché. The operator stands inside with his camera and the pictures are taken through a small hinged door. With this "property" dangerous animals can be approached closely.

Practical Cinematography

and its Applications

By

Frederick A. Talbot

Author of
"Moving Pictures" etc.

London   MCMXIII
William Heinemann

Many cow fa...
...d the picture...
...n be approached...

actical Cinematography

and its Applications

By

Frederick A. Talbot

Author of
" Moving Pictures " etc.

London   MCMXIII
William Heinemann

PREFACE

This volume has been written with the express purpose of assisting the amateur—the term is used in its broadest sense as a distinction from the salaried, attached professional worker—who is attracted towards cinematography. It is not a technical treatise, but is written in such a manner as to enable the tyro to grasp the fundamental principles of the art, and the apparatus employed in its many varied applications.

While it is assumed that the reader has practised ordinary snap-shot and still-life work, and thus is familiar with the elements of photography, yet the subject is set forth in such a manner as to enable one who never has attempted photography to take moving-pictures.

At the same time it is hoped that the volume may prove of use to the expert hand, by introducing him to what may be described as the higher branches of the craft. The suggestions and descriptions concerning these applications may prove of value to any who may be tempted to labour in one or other of the various fields mentioned.

285537

In the preparation of this volume I have received valuable assistance from several friends who have been associated intimately with the cinematographic art from its earliest days:— J. Bamberger, Esq., of the Motograph Company, Limited, James Williamson, Esq., of the Williamson Kinematograph Company, Limited, Kodak Limited, Messrs. Jury, Limited, and Monsieur Lucien Bull, the assistant-director of the Marey Institute, to whom I am especially indebted for facilities to visit that unique institution, and the investigation at first hand of its varied work, the loan of the photographs of the many experiments which have been, and still are being, conducted at the French " Cradle of Cinematography," and considerable assistance in the preparation of the text.

FREDERICK A. TALBOT.

CONTENTS

viii CONTENTS

LIST OF ILLUSTRATIONS

PRACTICAL CINEMATOGRAPHY

CHAPTER I

ATTRACTIONS AND OPPORTUNITIES OF THE ART

PROFIT and pleasure combine to win recruits for the art of animated photography. As an entertainment offered to the public, the moving-pictures have had no rival. Their popularity has been remarkable and universal. It increases daily, and, since we are only now beginning to see the magnitude of what the cinematograph can effect, it is not likely to diminish. This development has stirred the ambition of the amateur or independent photographer because the field is so vast, fertile, and promising. Remunerative reward is obtainable practically in every phase of endeavour so long as the elements of novelty or originality are manifest. The result is that it is attracting one and all. Animated photography can convey so fascinating and convincing a record of scenes and events that many persons—sportsmen, explorers, and travellers—make use of it.

From the commercial point of view the issue is one of magnetic importance. In all quarters there is an increasing demand for films of prominent topical interest, either of general or local significance. The proprietors of picture palaces have discovered that no films draw better audiences than these. If they deal with a prominent incident like a visit of royalty to the neighbourhood, an important sporting event, a public ceremony, or even, such is human nature, with some disaster to life or property, they will make a stronger appeal for a few days than the general film fare offered at the theatre, because the episode which is uppermost in the mind of the public is what draws and compels public attention. Even, it would seem, when the reality itself has just been witnessed by the audience, its photographic reproduction proves more attractive than all else.

The picture palace, indeed, is assuming the functions of the illustrated newspaper, and is governed by like laws. The more personal and immediate the news, the more pleased are the beholders. So there is an increasing effort to supply upon the screen in life and motion what the papers are recording in print and illustration. One can almost hear the phrase that will soon become general, "Animated news of the moment." Already the French are showing us the way. In Paris one is able to visit a picture palace for 25 centimes at any time between noon and midnight and see, upon the screen, the events of the hour in photographic action. As fresh items of news, or, rather, fresh sections of film, are received, they are thrown upon the screen in the pictorial equivalent of the paragraphs in the stop-press column of the newspapers, earlier items of less interest being condensed or expunged in the true journalistic manner to allow the latest photographic intelligence to be given in a length consistent with its importance.

It is obvious that this branch of the business must fall largely into the hands of the unattached or independent worker, who bears the same relation to the picture palace as the outside correspondent to the newspaper. A firm engaged in supplying topical films cannot hope to succeed without amateur assistance. No matter how carefully and widely it distributes its salaried photographers, numberless events of interest are constantly happening—shipwrecks, accidents, fires, sensational discoveries, movements of prominent persons, and the like, at places beyond the reach of the retained cinematographer. For film intelligence of these incidents the firm must rely upon the independent worker.

Curiously enough, in many cases, the amateur not only executes his work better than his salaried rival, but often outclasses him in the very important respect that he is more enterprising. Acting on his own responsibility, he knows that by smartness alone can he make way against professionals. Only by being the first to seize a chance can he find a market for his wares. Thus when Blériot crossed the English Channel in his aeroplane it was the camera of an amateur that caught the record of his flight for the picture palaces, although a corps of professionals was on the spot for the purpose. True, the successful film showed many defects. But defects matter little compared with the importance of getting the picture first or exclusively. Similar cases exist in plenty. The amateur has an excellent chance against the professional. His remuneration, too, is on a generous scale. The market is so wide and the competition is so keen, especially in London, which is the world's centre of the cinematograph industry, that the possessor of a unique film can dictate his own terms and secure returns often twenty times as great as the prime cost of the film he has used.

The market is open also to travellers, explorers, and sportsmen. These, with a cinematograph camera and a few thousand feet of film, can recompense themselves so well that the entire

By permission of the   Motograph Co.

A MOVING-PICTURE EXPEDITION INTO THE INDIAN JUNGLE.

Mr. Cherry Kearton, the famous cinematographer of wild animals, and his outfit loaded upon an elephant.

By permission of the   POLAR BEAR DIVING.   A STRIKING MOTION-PICTURE.   Motograph Co.

cost of an expedition may be defrayed. An Austrian sportsman who roamed and hunted in the North Polar icefields received over £6,000 ($30,000) for the films he brought back with him. Mr. Cherry Kearton, who took pictures of wild life in various parts of the world, sold his negatives for £10,000 or $50,000.

Scientific investigators are in the same happy case. When their researches lead them to anything that has an element of popular appeal, there is profit awaiting them at the picture palace. The life of the ant, for instance, or electrical experiments, or interesting phases of chemistry, and many other features of organic and inorganic science, yield good returns to the scientist with a camera. Such films will command 20s. ($5) or more per foot of negative.

There is another branch of the work already well established. The producer of picture plays, if his plot be tolerably good and the scenes well acted and well photographed, and if the play itself promises some popular success, can command a good price. At the moment there are several independent producers at work throughout the world. They have a large open market for the disposal of their wares and find no difficulty whatever in selling all they can produce. Even the largest producers, who have huge theatres and command the services of expert scenario writers and players, do not hesitate to purchase from outside sources.

A cinematograph camera, and a little luck, will make anyone's holiday profitable. The travelling amateur penetrates into places overlooked by the professional, and usually takes greater pains with his work. Afterwards he finds his market in the fact that the demand for travel pictures is so great that a good film of 300 feet will fetch £40 ($200) and upwards. At home he may exploit his ingenuity in making trick films, a most popular feature at the picture palaces, so long as he keeps novelty to the forefront. Trick films, unfortunately, take so long to prepare and demand such care, skill and patience that the largest firms of producers as a rule are not eager to attempt them, because their production disorganises the more regular and profitable work of the studio. A good trick film of 800 feet may occupy six months in preparation. But the amateur may approach what the large firm fears. To him time is no object, and he is able to maintain his interest, care, and ingenuity to the end of the quest. On the other hand the professional worker often tires of his trick subject before the task is half completed, with the result that novelty and care are not sustained. One industrious Frenchman devoted nearly a year to the preparation of a film in which resort had to be made to every conceivable form of trickery, and sold his product for £3,000 or $15,000. He also refused an offer of £5,000 ($25,000) for another film of pictures calculated to please children.

To sum up, the amateur or independent cinematographer has a vast field available for the profitable exercise of his skill. Except in regard to the topical work, which is of the rush-and-hustle order, he must show imagination in his choice of subject and craftsmanship in the execution of his work. He must, that is to say, be trained so far as to be no longer an amateur in the popular meaning of the word. He must learn aptitude in the school of experience. The reward is well worth the trouble.

Hitherto the amateur worker has been held back by the great expense of the necessary apparatus. The camera cost £50 ($250), and the developing and printing operations were generally supposed to be too difficult and costly for private undertaking. There was some excuse for these notions. The trade at first followed narrow lines, no welcome being held out to the amateur competitor. But circumstances have been too strong for this trade, as for others, and it burst its bonds in due time. The co-operation of the independent worker became essential as the demands of the market increased. In the production of plays, for instance, England at first led the way. But the American and French producers came quickly to the fore. The English pioneers, not being skilled in the mysteries of stage craft, wisely retired from the producing field upon the entrance of the expert from the legitimate theatre, who realised that the moving-picture field offered him increased opportunities for his knowledge and activity as well as bringing him more profitable financial returns for his labours. The British fathers of the industry devoted their energies to the manufacture of cinematographic apparatus, as they foresaw that sooner or later the amateur and independent worker must enter the industry. The activity of amateurs was needed by the English trade as a whole, and the manufacturer, with great enterprise, brought down the cost of apparatus to a very reasonable level. This has been effected by methods not less advantageous to the purchaser than is the reduction of the price—by standardisation of parts and simplification of mechanism.

To-day a reliable camera for living pictures, suitable for topical and other light work, can be bought for £5 or $25. A more expensive camera, the Williamson, costs £10 10s. ($52), and is actually as good as other machines priced at four or five times that sum. On the other hand, so much as £150 ($750) can be paid. But the camera sold for this large sum demands a purchaser with something more than a long purse. It demands special knowledge. Designed for studio work, it has peculiarities that are difficult to master and is not to be recommended to a beginner.

With the cost of the camera the cost of other apparatus has fallen in proportion. It was realised that the amateur's dark room and other facilities are likely to be less excellent than those of the professional and that he must be provided with compensating conveniences. This problem has been solved. A complete developing outfit can now be packed in a hand-bag, and a camera and printing outfit can be carried in a knapsack no larger than is required for the whole-plate camera of the old " still-life " photographer. Simple and efficient appliances for the dark room can be purchased very cheaply. There is a portable outfit for use in field work, where it is imperative that films should be developed as soon as possible after exposure, and this outfit is now used by the majority of travellers and field-workers, such as Cherry Kearton, Paul Rainey, and others. Distinct advantage, it may be observed, comes from prompt developing. There may be vexatious delay, occasionally, but the photographer is at least able to tell quickly whether his film is a success or a failure. It is better to gain this knowledge on the spot, even compulsorily, where another record can be taken, than to gain it later a few hundreds of miles from the chance of trying again.

The capital expenditure of the cinematographer need certainly not be great. A complete outfit, the "Jury," may now be obtained for £20 or $100. It comprises a combined camera and printer, developing troughs, film-winding frames for developing and drying, and all necessary chemicals. Yet it is no toy, as might be thought, but a thoroughly reliable outfit capable of doing first-class work. Anyone who is more ambitious, or willing to spend more money, should purchase the Williamson outfit. This costs about £40, or $200.

Now for other difficulties that have nothing to do with money. It has been assumed that the art of animated photography is a mystery demanding a long and weary apprenticeship. But the impression is really quite wrong. Anyone who has practised still-life and snap-shot photography may become proficient in the new art within a week or two. Many of the problems encountered in the old photography are actually easier to solve in the new; some are eliminated entirely; others, that are intensified, are really not very hard to master.

Animated photography is nothing more than a Kodak worked by machinery. Instead of the shutter being actuated by hand to make an

A LION AND LIONESS AT LUNCH.

CAUGHT!

A jungle-fowl brought down by a leopard.

exposure, and the film afterwards moved by turning a roller so as to bring a fresh area before the lens, the two movements, in the cinematograph, are combined. The rotation of the handle alternately opens and closes the lens, and moves the film forward a defined distance after each exposure. Therefore, speaking generally, if the beginner knows how to use an ordinary camera and is familiar with subsequent operations of developing and printing, he should be able to accustom himself quite readily, with little waste of material, to the different conditions of motion photography.

There is practically but one process that he should not at first attempt. This is the perforation of the film. The film is a celluloid ribbon and is punctured near either edge, at intervals, so as to enable it to be gripped by the claws of the mechanism and moved forward intermittently a definite distance—three quarters of an inch—through the camera. This puncturing or perforation of the film is the most delicate of the whole cycle of operations. It can only be done by a machine of unerring precision manipulated with extreme care. The machines, though many are on the market, are somewhat expensive, and it is upon them that the steadiness of the picture on the screen depends. The inaccuracy in the perforation may be slight, a minute fraction of an inch, but it must be remembered that each picture on the film is magnified more than fifteen thousand times upon the screen, and the errors are magnified in proportion. But these considerations need not trouble the amateur. He can purchase his "stock," as the unexposed film is called, perforated ready for use.

In spite of the great reduction in the cost of both camera and outfit the expense of cinematography is still its drawback. The film is the culprit. It costs from 2d. to 4d.—say, from 4 to 10 cents—a foot. Yet in this case, as in others, reduction seems to be within sight. The increased demand is sure to cheapen the process of production. If the price is not then lowered as much as could be hoped the cause will be in the cost of the basic materials. These also, perhaps, will become less dear in time. Cinematography is an industry in revolution. Its possibilities are only beginning to be seen; its followers are only beginning to be counted; but it can hardly be doubted that the ranks of the amateur and independent workers are certain to increase considerably and rapidly. The attractions and inducements to practise the craft are too alluring to be ignored.

CHAPTER II

THE PRINCIPLES OF CINEMATOGRAPHY

For complete success in moving-picture work it is essential to have an elementary knowledge of the principles upon which the art is based. Although pictures are said to be shown in motion upon the screen, no action is reproduced as a matter of fact. The eye imagines that it sees movement. Each picture is an isolated snap-shot taken in the fraction of a second. In projection upon the screen, however, the images follow so rapidly one after the other and each remains in sight for so brief a period that the successive views dissolve into one another. The missing parts of the motion —the parts lost while the lens is closed between the taking of each two pictures—are not detected by the eye. The latter imagines that it sees the whole of the process of displacement in the moving objects. In fact it sees only one-half— the half that occurred in those fractions of seconds during which the lens was open. What occurred while the lens was shut is not recorded. Animated photography, therefore, is an optical illusion purely and simply.

The fact that an appearance of natural movement is seen under these conditions is due to a physiological phenomenon which, for the want of a better explanation, is termed "persistence of vision." This peculiarity of the eye and brain remains a scientific puzzle, and although in one or two quarters the theory of visual persistence is ridiculed, the iconoclasts have not yet brought conclusive testimony to upset it. The whole subject of persistence of vision in its relation to moving-pictures is discussed at length by the present writer in a former book to which he would refer such readers as may wish for information on this subject.[1]

The eye is about one million times faster than the most rapid sensitized emulsion which chemists have yet produced. So there is nothing wrong about the popular opinion that the organ of sight is the quickest of the senses. Yet it is not so quick that it cannot be deceived. If the pictures of a cinematograph are projected upon the screen at the rate of so many per second, the effect upon the eye is that of perfectly natural movement. The laws that govern this illusion have been discovered in a very interesting way. A positive film was prepared, but between each successive image a wide white

[1] See "Moving Pictures: How they are made and worked," Chapter I.

OPERATOR AND HIS CAMERA BURIED IN A HOLE TO TAKE
MOVING-PICTURES OF SMALL ANIMALS.

By permission of the   *Motograph Co.*

MAKING MOVING-PICTURES OF WILD RABBITS.

Mr. Frank Newman with his camera concealed in the bushes.

Motograph Co.

A Unique Picture. The Mother King Regulus Feeding her Young.

From the "Cinema College," by permission of the

The Nest, showing Curious Suspension by Four Strings.

Motion-pictures of the Golden-crested Wren, the smallest bird in the British Isles.

line was inscribed. This film was then passed through the projector, and the pictures were thrown upon the screen at the speed generally accepted as being necessary to convey the effect of natural movement; but animation could not be produced at all, however rapidly the pictures were projected. The reason was simple. Immediately after a picture disappeared from the screen the white flash occurred, and notwithstanding its instantaneous character it was sufficient to wipe out the image of the picture, which without the white line would have lingered in the brain. Even when the pictures were run through the projector at thirty per second, no impression of rhythmic movement was obtained; they appeared in the form of still-life pictures with spasmodic jumps from one to the other. They failed to blend or dissolve in the brain, notwithstanding that the white flash in some cases was only about one ten thousandth part of a second in duration.

Another film of the same subject then was passed through the projector under conditions exactly similar except that the line dividing the pictures in this case was black instead of white. When this picture was thrown upon the screen, animation became apparent directly the speed attained sixteen pictures per second, because after one image had vanished from the screen it persisted in the brain, in spite of the black flash, until the next picture appeared.   Thus, the requisite dissolving effect was obtained.   The black flash did indeed produce a defect like that which was common in the early days of cinematography and was characterised generally as "flicker."   But it did not suffice to ruin the illusion of movement.   A white flash destroys apparent motion, owing to the brain being extremely sensitive to white : a black flash of equal duration exercises no ill effects.

In the latest development of the art, one inventor has taken advantage of this peculiarity. He has perfected a practical system wherewith the shutter of the camera may be abandoned because each picture is cut off from its neighbour by a very thin black line.   An improved mechanism jerks each picture off and brings the next one on the screen very sharply, so that an effect is produced like that obtainable with the shutter and without any impression of flicker. It may be pointed out that with this invention there are none of the aberrations described in a later chapter, such as the spokes of a wheel appearing to move in the reverse direction to which which the rim is travelling.

The next question is that of the speed at which it is necessary to take and to project the pictures in order to get an apparently true impression of natural movement.   This factor to-day is governed almost entirely by commercial considerations. It has been found, as a result of elaborate investigation, that a speed of twelve to sixteen pictures per second is the minimum wherewith in monochrome pictures animation is obtainable. But this applies only to general work, such as records of ordinary scenes, topical events and stage plays, where the action of the moving objects is comparatively slow. In these instances an average of sixteen pictures per second in photographing and projecting gives completely satisfactory effects.

But in reality the speed is a variable quantity : it must be adapted to the subject and the character of the work in hand. In other words, strictly speaking, the speed must be accommodated to the velocity of the subject so far as photographing is concerned, and also, in a lesser degree, to the distance of the moving object from the lens. For instance, when a man, walking four miles an hour, is photographed at sixteen pictures per second, the movements recorded are far from being natural or rhythmic. On the screen he appears to walk with a disjointed action. To obtain a lifelike result, his pace should be slowed down 75 per cent., or the photographing speed should be accelerated to seventy pictures per second at the least. This fact is illustrated very conclusively in pictures of soldiers marching : they appear to

advance like automatons. Again, in photographing animals, a complete movement is often lost
between successive pictures. A cat in one picture will be seen to the right ; in the next picture
it is on the left, having sprung from one side to
the other during the brief interval the lens
was closed. When extremely rapid movements
have to be recorded, the photographing speed has
to be accelerated to an extreme degree, up to ten
thousand pictures or more per second in the case of
a bullet leaving the muzzle of a rifle, and up to two
thousand pictures per second to catch the movements of a dragon-fly's wings. On the other
hand, in photographing very slow movements
like the growth of a plant, one picture per hour
may be adequate.

In projection the speed can be adjusted. The
ten thousand pictures per second may be decelerated to sixteen per second to allow the
movement to be followed, and although the rifle
bullet may appear to crawl through the air, the
movement is perfectly correct. Similarly the
very slow motions must be accelerated to sixteen
pictures per second to obtain evident animation. These two extreme phases of cinematographic investigation are described at length in
another part of this volume, but are mentioned
here merely to show that the photographing
speed is a somewhat elastic factor, to be adapted

to circumstances in order to produce passably natural effects.

For everyday work, however, a speed of sixteen pictures per second is sufficient and represents the generally practised velocity. Possibly in the near future the speed will be accelerated to twenty, twenty-two, or twenty-four pictures per second, as the present speed is generally admitted to be too slow. The eyes of the regular picture palace patrons have become trained, as it were, with the result that there is an appreciable strain of the eyes, while the disjointed character of the movements on the screen may be detected. But when the taking and projecting speed is accelerated by 50 per cent. the picture stands steadier upon the screen, the movements are more natural, and there is an entire absence of that automaton effect which is so characteristic of most pictures taken under prevailing conditions. These considerations do not affect photo-plays produced in the studio so materially, because there the actions of the players can be slowed down to suit the conditions.

One of the leading manufacturers is earnestly considering the advisability of accelerating the taking and projecting speeds up to about twenty pictures per second, and private investigations and experiments have certainly demonstrated the value of such an improvement. Unfortunately

two difficulties prevent its immediate realisation.
An increase of only four pictures per second
represents an increase of 25 per cent. in the consumption of the film, and therefore in its cost.
The other difficulty is more serious. Existing
apparatus, both cameras and projectors, are geared
to eight pictures per turn of the handle. This
involves two complete revolutions per second.
Consequently the gearing of the mechanism would
have to be altered, and this is a more trouble-
some question than appears at first sight. Some
time may elapse before a forward step is taken
in this direction. In matters of this character
the cinematograph industry is notoriously conservative, although the moment one firm courage-
ously adopts an accelerated speed, the higher
quality of the resulting pictures will force the
others to follow the example.

As a matter of fact the decision to adopt sixteen
pictures per second was taken somewhat hap-
hazardly without any scientific investigation.
When it became standardised, film was expensive.
Accordingly, efforts were made to secure the
requisite effect with the minimum expenditure
of film. Machines were built to coincide with
these requirements, and the original designs have
been followed slavishly in their broad outlines
ever since.

CHAPTER III

THE cinematograph camera differs entirely from the instruments used in other branches of photography. While the advanced worker and the prosperous picture-play producer employ costly and elaborate machines, the amateur, or the independent worker, in the particular field which he has selected for his operations, can get equally good results with an apparatus only a fifteenth or even a twentieth part as expensive. The range of operation with the cheaper instrument may be limited, and it may be deficient in those many little refinements which are characteristic of the professional appliance, and may lack silver-plated finish and highly-polished woodwork or morocco leather covering. But the camera itself is more important than these.

The cameras, both expensive and low-priced, work upon the same fundamental principles. In the latter everything is reduced to the simplest form so as to be readily and easily understood by the beginner. They have the additional recommendation that the risk of breakdown is eliminated, because the few essential component parts are substantially made, well-proportioned, and nicely-balanced. Serviceability and reliability are the outstanding features of the low-priced camera, and it is applicable to almost every branch of the craft.

Contrary to general belief, taking the "movies" is quite as simple as snap-shot photography with a Kodak. In the latter case you press the button ; in the former you turn the handle; the camera does the rest. The rotation of the handle, a simple operation, performs every duty through the internal mechanism. It swings the shutter across the lens, moves the film intermittently through the instrument, and coils up the exposed film in its dark box.

As has been explained, the beginner is now able to make his selection from a wide variety of makes, ranging in price from £5 ($25) upwards. If one desires to gain experience in the cinematographic art with the minimum capital outlay, the Jury, "New Era," or "Alpha" cameras will suit the purpose excellently. Both are first-class, well-made machines, having perfect registration and alignment, extremely simple and easy to handle. The first-named model, which is the cheapest, is contained in a mahogany case measuring $9\frac{1}{2}$ inches square by $4\frac{3}{4}$ inches deep, and in the unloaded condition weighs $5\frac{1}{4}$ pounds. The "Alpha," which costs a little more, is full value for money, and is well worth the slightly increased price.   This camera is fitted with a light-proof hinged front panel giving access to the adjustable shutter, which permits the opening of the latter to be varied within wide limits and thus enables extremely rapid movements to be photographed while running the machine at the normal speed. The spool boxes carry 100 feet of film of standard gauge in each instance, and for general all-round work, such as the recording of topical events, either model will be found perfectly efficient.   It may be mentioned that both models are supplied without the lens, because the average beginner in motion-picture work, having practised still-life or snap-shot photography, has usually developed a marked fancy for some particular make of lens —Dallmeyer, Cooke, Ross, Zeiss-Tessar, or Voigtlander.   Naturally, being familiar with the working of his favourite and knowing what he can do with it, he feels more at home when he is able to have it fitted to his moving-picture machine.   Here, again, there is a wide selection to meet all purses, so that the most fastidious tastes in regard to the lens may be gratified.   On the other hand, if the beginner has no marked preference, and wishes to be economical, he can get a lens capable of doing first-class work at a remarkably low price.   His complete outlay upon the camera and the lens need not exceed £6 5s., or, say, $31.

If prices are not to be so strictly considered, and if the beginner wishes to have a machine of the finest type at a comparatively low figure, he cannot do better than fit himself out with a Williamson camera, the price of which, complete with lens, is £10 10s., say $52. Except for an expert, it is difficult to detect the difference between this machine and one which costs five times as much, for both are designed upon the same lines, are equally well made, and equally capable of doing the finest work. It must not be forgotten that Mr. James Williamson, the designer of the latter instrument, was one of the pioneers in cinematography, and, in his machine, the results of some twenty-five years varied and accumulated experience are incorporated. He has been able to realise just those essentials which are required for a high-class apparatus free from complexity, and this end has been achieved to excellent effect. The camera, finished in a brass-bound mahogany or teak case—the latter is preferable for working in tropical countries — measures 9½ inches square by 4¾ inches deep, is fitted with a Zeiss-Tessar 2-inch lens with focussing, and iris diaphragm. It weighs 7½ pounds complete in loaded condition. It is eminently suited for all round duties, from

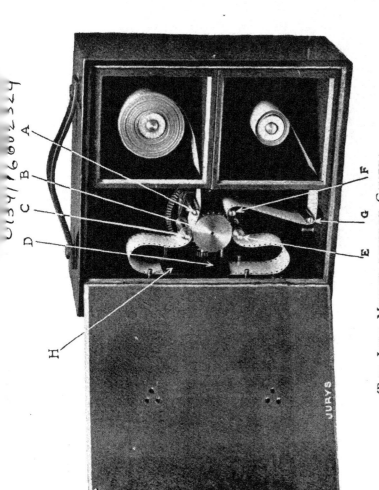

THE JURY MOVING-PICTURE CAMERA. A, C. Upper sprocket pulleys. D. Exposure
window. H. Gate. E, F. Lower sprocket pulleys. G. Exposed film-
box guide pulley. B. Driving sprocket.

THE WILLIAMSON TOPICAL CAMERA AND TRIPOD.

A. Camera.   B. Handle.   C. Lens.   D. View finder.
E. Tripod head. F. Horizontal panoramic movement handle.
G. Vertical panoramic movement handle.

the rush and tumble of topical work to the uneventful, quiet but exacting requirements of the laboratory.

These machines by no means exhaust the selection. Other manufacturers have produced very good instruments at competitive prices, but those which I have mentioned represent probably the best in their respective classes. For the purpose of introduction to the art of cinematography the beginner can do no better than obtain one of them. If, after a little experience, he comes to the conclusion that he has ventured into the wrong province, then his monetary expenditure is not serious.

It will be seen that the aspirant has no lack of inducement to embark upon the moving-picture industry. Provided he has acquired a certain knowledge of the elements of photography, and is possessed of average intelligence, there is no reason why he should not be able to produce pictures with his inexpensive machine that are in all ways comparable with the product of the professional worker and the costly instrument. Naturally, as the intricacies of the craft are mastered, the tyro will wish for a more elaborate apparatus. He can gratify his ambitions in accordance with his progress, or with the improvement in his financial position.

The mechanism of the modern cinematograph

camera is very simple in its character and very easy to understand. The necessary parts are very few in number. In all cameras the chief object is to effect the forward intermittent movement of the film at regular intervals and for a defined distance. For this purpose the early types of camera were fitted with what is known as the Geneva stop movement. Opinion is divided upon its merits, some authorities condemning it unequivocably, while others uphold it strenuously, contending that it gives a steadier and freer motion. There is much to be said in favour of the latter view. Mechanically the Geneva stop movement is perfect. So far as cinematography is concerned its advantages were proved most emphatically by Mr. Robert Paul, the first man to bring motion pictures into commercial application in Great Britain. He adopted this movement in his camera, and it cannot be denied that his pictures were in every way equal to those produced to-day, while his camera has never been excelled. Curiously enough, although this movement has been superseded, there is a tendency among expert workers to revive it, and many cameras specially built have been fitted with it.

The movement more commonly used is that known as the "claw." It is simple, and has the advantage of bringing the film into place for an

exposure with a sharp, quick jerk. But it is a movement which requires to be designed very finely
in order to perform its work smoothly and evenly,
and without inflicting any injury upon the film.

The claw consists of a small lever in duplicate,
which is so mounted as to have an eccentric
movement and is driven direct by the main gear
wheel rotated by the handle. The free upper
end of each arm of the lever has a projecting
pointed tooth of sufficient size to engage with the
perforations on either side of the film. With
the revolution of the wheel upon which it is
mounted eccentrically the claw engages with the
perforations, and, thus gripping the film after
the manner of a ratchet and pawl, jerks it
downwards a definite distance. When this
downward movement is completed the claw
disengages from the perforations and falls back
clear of the film. Then the wheel, continuing
its rotary movement, proceeds to lift the claw.
When it has raised it to its highest point
it brings it forward smartly to re-engage
with the perforations, and causes a fresh downward movement of the film. The action is
intermittent and occurs at regular intervals, while
the movement of the film is always the same.
Quick engagement and disengagement of the
perforations is imperative for preventing the
vibration and tearing of the film.

The mechanism of the camera may be understood from the diagram (Fig. 1), which refers to the Williamson instrument. The sprocket A is driven directly by the operating handle, which engages with the sprocket spindle. This

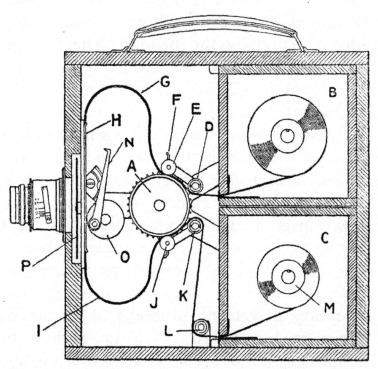

FIG. 1.—Mechanism of camera showing threading of film.

sprocket A is fitted with two rows of teeth, mounted upon its periphery, and so spaced apart, both circumferentially and transversely, as to coincide with the distances between the perforations of the film. A pair of twin rollers, D and E, bear against this sprocket under the tension of a spring, their object being to keep the film pressed firmly against the sprocket. The teeth engage with the film perforations, so that by the rotation of the handle and sprocket the film is fed forwards regularly, smoothly and evenly, as it is drawn from the loaded spool box B.

The film is brought into position before the lens by passing through what is known as the "gate." This device H consists of two parts of which the first is fixed irremovably while the second is hinged to the first at one side and kept flat against it by means of a spring. Both of the parts are provided with an aperture or window, the exact size of a cinematograph picture—1 inch wide by $\frac{3}{4}$-inch deep—through which the light passes, after admission through the lens, to strike upon the sensitized surface of the film. There is just sufficient space between the two parts of the gate to permit the film to move easily, and its object is to hold the film perfectly flat and steady during the period of exposure. Each picture is thus kept in absolute focus.

The feed through the gate is accomplished by the claw N, which is mounted upon the eccentric O as already described. At the instant of exposure the claw is free of the film, or in the "out position," as it is termed, so that the sensitized ribbon is absolutely still. When an exposure has been made, the claw, having risen to the highest point of its travel, re-engages with the film and jerks it down ¾ inch, so as to bring a fresh unexposed surface before the lens. As the film emerges from the gate it is picked up once more by the sprocket A, the engagement of the perforations in the film with the sprocket teeth being assured by the two rollers J and K. The film then passes under the guide roller L, and is wound up on the bobbin M in the exposed film box C, the bobbin being worked through the handle that drives the mechanism.

The rotation of the handle also ensures, through gearing, the revolution of the shutter P, whereby the lens is eclipsed intermittently. The shutter is a ring fitted with an opaque sector which comes before the lens and shuts out the light during the movement of the film through the gate H by the claw N. In the Williamson camera this shutter is recessed into the case.

Although the lens may be of the fixed focus class—the focussing distance varying with the stop used—focussing can be carried out independently if very critical work is required. In the case of the Williamson camera and others of this type, focussing is accomplished by opening the shutter and the side of the camera and looking through the gate. In some cameras a focussing tube is provided. This passes from the gate to

the rear of the instrument, through a space provided between the superimposed film dark-boxes.
It is telescopic at the forward end.   Thus, when
focussing is being carried out, it can be extended
so as to come flush with the gate, and pushed
back out of the way when all is ready for working,
so that the free movement of the film is not
obstructed in any way.   The rear end of the
tube, which extends through the rear face of
the camera box, is fitted with a cap to save the
film from being fogged by light entering from
behind.

One conspicuous advantage of the Williamson
machine is that the whole of the mechanism is
mounted upon a skeleton casting fixed to the
interior of the mahogany case by means of four
screws.   By withdrawing these the whole of the
internal mechanism may be removed intact, and
much trouble is saved when inspection or repairs
are necessary.

In some cameras the intermittent movement of
the film is effected by a single claw which engages
with the perforations upon one side of the film
only.   But this movement is not perfect.   All the
pulling strain is thrown upon one side of the
film.   This gives it a tendency to move unevenly
into the gate and also increases the risk of
tearing.

The driving gear of the camera is so adjusted

that one complete revolution of the handle completes eight exposures. Consequently two revolutions have to be made per second to maintain the necessary speed of sixteen pictures per second. In the Williamson camera this is emphasised as a fixed speed in ordinary working, and any compensations demanded by the varying intensity of the light are made by altering the aperture of the lens. This is a logical method, for if the operator is required to make such compensations by varying the speed of his handle he is apt to obtain an indifferent result. It requires a very skilled operator indeed to vary the speed of the handle with judgment between the narrow limits possible. In some cameras this compensation for light is effected by varying the area of the opaque section of the shutter, but this is not so simple or effective a method as the variation of the stop. The latter can be accomplished while the camera is being driven, but in the former it is necessary that the work should be stopped while the front panel camera is opened and the shutter adjusted.

As for the tripod, one cannot be too careful in choosing it. This apparently insignificant detail has a far-reaching effect upon the picture results. Any ordinary tripod used in photographic work may suffice, but its absolute rigidity is essential. A tight head, too, is most necessary, without which the operator will get a side-to-side sway upon the picture. It must be borne in mind that in turning the handle there is a tendency, especially at first, to exert an unequal pressure upon the handle side of the camera, and, unless the support and its head are kept absolutely rigid, the pictures will betray evidences of the defect. The telescopic ladder tripod is very handy for topical work. This, when it is extended and when the camera is fixed, brings the lens some 7 feet above the ground. A cross-rail placed from 12 to 25 inches above the ground, and attached to the rear legs, offers a platform upon which the operator can stand to work his instrument. In this way both camera and operator are brought above the heads of the crowd, and an uninterrupted view can be obtained.

For moving-picture work a special type of tripod head has been evolved, which allows the camera to be moved bodily through both the horizontal and the vertical planes while exposures are being made. Thus it can follow a subject travelling in either of these directions. The movements are upon the rack and pinion principle, a small handle being fitted to each motion so that either can be operated independently of the other. By means of this panoramic attachment the main object in the picture, such as a carriage or an aeroplane, may be followed in either direction. But if both movements are to be completed simultaneously, the operator will require help. One person must sight the object and keep it in the picture by the manipulation of the two handles governing the respective movements of the tripod head, while the other confines his energies to turning the camera handle.

Although the moving-picture camera is built substantially and strongly, its mechanism is comparatively delicate. While it will withstand the hardest descriptions of legitimate work, it succumbs readily to brutal treatment. Although operated by means of a handle, it is neither a coffee mill nor a barrel organ, but a sensitive scientific instrument, and it must be treated as such if the finest results are to be obtained. Rough usage will throw out the registration and alignment. If handled carefully a camera should perform its task for years without needing repair. The effects of wear and tear can be mitigated very appreciably by keeping the moving parts well lubricated with good oil, such as is used for clocks, which neither gums nor clogs the bearings, nor injures the mechanism in any way.

CHAPTER IV

THE CAMERA AND HOW TO USE IT

HAVING examined the mechanism of the moving-picture camera, and the broad principles upon which it works, we must now study the way to use it.

The first step is to load the film box, an operation which must be carried out in the dark room. The film is sold as a rule in standardised lengths, such as 100, 200, 350 feet, etc. With the ordinary type of camera the 100 or 200 feet lengths are used. For topical work either are quite adequate as a rule.

As has been said, the film is supplied perforated and ready for use. Many firms that sell the "stock," as the unexposed film is called, attach a blank or unsensitized "lead" to one end of the roll, for the purpose of "threading-up" the camera. If this is not supplied, and if the operator wishes to avoid the waste of 2 or 3 feet of sensitized ribbon, the deficiency can easily be remedied. For the blank "lead" all that is required is about 3 feet of useless or spoiled film which, however, should not be torn or cracked.   The emulsion at one end of this should be scraped off for a distance of about $\frac{1}{4}$ inch.   A pocket knife will do this very efficiently.   The blank should then be laid flat upon the table, emulsion side uppermost, preferably upon a sheet of glass which secures a smooth, clean, level surface, and a little film cement applied to the scraped end of the blank.   Film cement can be obtained readily and cheaply in small bottles complete with cap and brush.   A bottle should always be kept to hand as it is often required, especially in joining up successive lengths of film; but if it should so happen that none is available at the moment, glacial acetic acid may be used with equal success, although it demands more careful handling.   In an emergency alcohol constitutes a first-class cement, but it requires extreme care and skill because it is a solvent of the celluloid base.

After the cement has been applied to the cleaned end of the blank lead, the end of the unexposed coil of film is laid upon it, emulsion side uppermost, the overlap being about $\frac{3}{4}$ inch. Care must be exercised to see that the joint is made perfectly square and that the perforation holes of each piece of film come dead true, otherwise there will be trouble in passing the joint through the camera mechanism.   When it has been superimposed satisfactorily, pressure must be applied to secure perfect adhesion. In order to ensure perfect jointing a film jointer should be used: in fact it is an indispensable and inexpensive tool.

When attaching the blank lead every precaution must be taken to protect the spool of unexposed film from light ; only a very faint ruby glow should be used, for the cinematograph film is extremely sensitive. The cement dries rapidly, and the joint being found to be perfect the dark box should then be loaded. The coil of ribbon is slipped over the central bobbin. A hole large enough for this purpose is always left in the coil. The end of the lead is then passed through the velvet-faced slot near the bottom of the box. In order to prevent the loose end slipping back into the box, in which event there must be another journey to the dark room, it should be bent back and re-entered into the slot so as to form an external loop. The dark box is then closed, and securely locked, and is ready for insertion in the camera. It is advisable to carry at least two loaded boxes, especially if each is only of 100 or 200 feet capacity. The camera is provided with two dark boxes, one placed above the other. The upper box carries the unexposed film, while the lower receives the ribbon after exposure.

The camera may then be "threaded-up," or, if focussing is desired, this can be completed first.

With the Williamson camera focussing is unnecessary within certain distances owing to the
fixed foci of the stops. These will be explained
later. Many other manufacturers of cameras
follow the same principle, and it is most convenient for every-day work. Yet it may happen
that the operator desires to focus critically. In
this event he opens the side of the camera, lifts
the pressure plate of the gate, and inserts into
the gate window a small length, about 2 inches,
of matt film, with the matt side towards the lens.
The matt film serves exactly the same purpose
as the ground-glass in the ordinary plate camera.
The handle is revolved until the lens is opened,
and the image thrown upon the matt film becomes
apparent. This can then be focussed by moving
the milled focussing screw on the lens until the
picture stands out as sharply as is desired. At
first the operation may appear to be somewhat
awkward, because the operator has to look upon
the matt film at an angle. It is easier in the case
of a camera fitted with a focussing tube, for the
operator has then merely to open the side of the
machine to insert the matt film and push the
telescopic tube out to its fullest extent to bear
against the gate. By removing the cap from the
tube upon the rear face of the camera, and
looking through it as if through a telescope, he
is able to look squarely upon his screen.

When focussing is complete the matt film is withdrawn and placed in a safe position. It is a good plan to clinch it to the bottom inner surface of the camera with drawing pins, for it can then be found when it is wanted. Should the piece be lost the defect can be repaired as follows. Take a small bit of waste film; scrape off the gelatine emulsion; and rough the celluloid surface with a piece of sandpaper; or even with a rough stone surface. It is well to carry a few inches of spoiled film in the pocket for such an emergency.

The film may now be threaded up. The loop of blank projecting from the dark box is picked up and the coil within is steadily unwound as the threading proceeds. The blank is first passed under the pressure roller (marked D in Fig. 1), and then under the spring roller E, which can be lifted for this purpose. It must be seen that the teeth of the sprocket engage with the perforations in the film. A loop G is then made and the film is threaded through the gate H. Before this can be done the claw N must be thrown in the "out" position to obtain access to the gate, which is done by turning round the eccentric. The spring part of the gate is then opened on its hinge, and the film is slipped in from the side. Care must be observed that an ample loop is left above the gate. When the gate is closed once more another loop I similar to that above the gate, is formed. The film now is passed round the under side of the sprocket A, the spring roller J being pressed back to admit of easy entrance, and the end of the blank is passed under the second or pressure roller K. Here again one must be careful to see that the insertion is square and that the sprocket teeth mesh with the film perforations. The film is then carried under guide roller L and through the velvet-faced slit into the empty film box C. This must be opened to permit the free end of the lead to be secured to the centre bobbin M, on which the film is wound in after exposure. The handle should be given a few turns to see that threading has been carried out properly, and also that it is properly attached to the bobbin M. If a sufficient length of blank is attached to the end of the unexposed film, and a piece of gummed paper is fixed on the lead about 6 inches in advance of the joint, it is possible to continue winding in on the lower bobbin until this mark appears at the mouth of the loaded dark box.

If the threading has been accomplished properly the interior of the camera should be as shown in the illustration facing p. 42. Here both film boxes are shown open, though of course the upper one is kept closed during the threading process. The most important part of this operation is the formation of ample loops both above and below the gate. Once formed they remain constant, because of the action of the teeth on the sprocket; for the movement of the ribbon over the sprocket is equal to that produced by the claws through the gate. At first sight the necessity of these loops may not be apparent, but when it is remembered that the film is moved through the gate intermittently, sixteen times per second, with a vicious jerk, it will be seen that if there were no loop, and the film were drawn directly from the dark box, a great strain would be imposed upon it, and probably it would break. But by providing the loop an elastic feed is secured, and the film is jerked into position before the lens with the minimum of vibration and without any risk of tearing or displacement.

Threading completed the lower dark box is closed and secured, together with the side of the camera, so that the whole of the interior is light-proof. The camera should not be re-opened after photographing has commenced until the whole of the film in the loaded box is exhausted, or, if the supply is not used, until the dark-room is regained, unless the waste of a foot or two of film is a secondary consideration. Should it become necessary to open the camera in the field, the handle should be given two or three turns to make sure that the last picture taken is wound into the exposed film box and is thus secure from the light. Opening the side of the camera obviously ruins the whole of the unexposed film threaded through the mechanism, so that when picture taking is resumed the handle must be given a few more turns to make sure that the whole of the light-ruined film has passed through the gate. Seeing that one turn of the handle represents eight exposures, equivalent to 6 inches of film, it is a simple matter to estimate how many turns of the handle are necessary to clear the gate of spoiled film.

Most cameras are provided with a film indicator enabling the operator to tell at a glance how many feet of film have been exposed. In this case, care must be taken to see that the indicator is returned to zero when the mechanism is threaded-up.

Another convenience is the "punch" whereby it is possible to mark the film after an incident has been photographed, so that the worker can afterwards tell in the dark room by a mere touch where the exposure ended in each case, The film should be marked after every episode is finished because it is then possible, if desired, to develop the film in lengths. Indeed it is advisable to follow this practice, and especially when the exposures have been made under varying conditions of light. By developing in sections

THE WILLIAMSON CAMERA THREADED READY FOR USE.

The film is taken from the upper unexposed film-box, passed over the sprocket, through the gate, under the sprocket and wound into the lower exposed film-box.

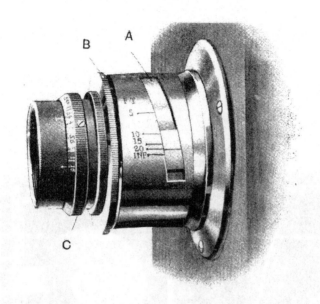

THE LENS OF THE WILLIAMSON CAMERA.
(For explanation see p. 43.)

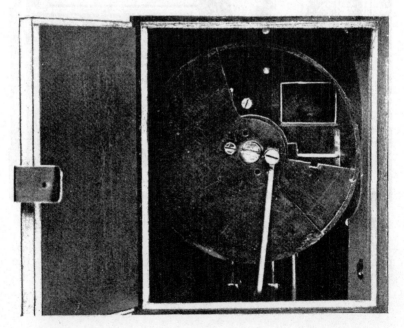

THE ADJUSTABLE SHUTTER OF THE JURY CAMERA.

one gets lengths of uniform density—a great assistance in printing.

In cinematography, as in ordinary photography, the judgment of the brilliance of the light and of the right stop to use on each occasion, is the one important factor for which mechanical provision is impossible. This is because of the extreme variation of the light conditions. But, while no hard and fast rules concerning exposure can be laid down, it is possible to give the beginner a little guidance to keep him on the safe side. Practice alone can make perfect, and experience is the more necessary because the cinematograph is an all-the-year-round machine. In topical work the operator is compelled to make the most of the existing weather conditions, no matter how deplorable they may be.

Under these circumstances it is well to have what might be termed a very flexible lens. The lens, that is to say, should be fitted with the means of varying the size of the aperture, and varying it within wide limits, according to the light conditions. The simplest way of achieving this is by means of what is called an iris diaphragm.

To illustrate the functions of the iris diaphragm we will take the Williamson instrument. This is fitted with a Zeiss-Tessar lens of 2-inch focus. By the aid of the iris diaphragm the diameter of the aperture may be varied from approximately ⅜ to ⅛ of an inch. Now it is obvious that more light can be passed through the lens with the larger, than with the smaller, aperture. While the larger aperture would do excellently for filming a football match on a dull day in mid-winter, it would be useless for a seascape on a cloudless day in July. For the latter the smallest aperture would suffice. But the requirements between these two extremes must be met: in other words the aperture must be adapted to intermediate demands. By turning the milled ring in which the iris diaphragm is mounted the size of the aperture can be varied even to a minute degree and thus adjusted to any sort of light conditions. For the guidance of the operator the total rotary travel of the ring is graduated to six different definite points or as many different sized apertures. These are as follows :—

$f/3.5$ gives an aperture ⅜-inch in diameter (nearly)

4	,,	,,	½-inch	,,
5·6	,,	,,	⅓-inch	,, ,,
8	,,	,,	¼-inch	,,
11	,,	,,	⅕-inch	,, ,,
16	,,	,,	⅛-inch	,,

Although the differences between these successive apertures are very slight, they exercise a very appreciable effect upon the volume of light passing through the lens, and accordingly the period of the exposure. Thus although stop $f/5\cdot6$ only decreases the size of the aperture by $\frac{1}{8}$ of an inch over $f/4$, yet the effect of this reduction is to necessitate twice as long an exposure as is suited for the latter stop. Similarly $f/8$ demands twice the exposure of that required for $f/5\cdot6$, and so on, the exposure being doubled with every diminution of the stop up to the limits of the diaphragm. Yet in practice this increase of exposure between two stops is impossible, because the handle must be turned at a definite speed. It is obvious, therefore, that compensation must come from another quarter. Instead of increasing the duration of the exposure we must have a greater intensity of light for $f/5\cdot6$ than for $f/4$.

At first sight the beginner might be disposed to think that the selection of the most favourable aperture is a matter demanding extremely fine judgment and skill, especially when there are other factors which may upset calculations. Many other advantages arise from using as small an aperture as possible, such as increased sharpness of the picture, especially at the edges. Mr. Williamson the designer of the camera has realised this, and as a result of his unique experience, he has set down some very useful rules to guide the beginner, as to which stop should be used for varying conditions of light and subject. In elaborating this advice Mr. Williamson rightly commences from the zero point as it were, taking moving-pictures of a football match on a dull winter afternoon, when, owing to the feeble light, the capacity of the lens and the sensitiveness of the film are strained to the utmost. From this point he has graduated the diaphragm and its use as follows :—

Stop.	Subject and Conditions.
F/3·5	On a dull winter's day ; well-lighted interior : or on a subject at any time of the year where there are heavy shadows such as under trees.
F/4	On a bright day in winter : on dull days in spring and autumn.
F/5·6	Outdoor exposures during September, October, March, and April. Dull summer weather.
F/8	Street scenes in bright summer weather.
F/11	Open fields in bright sunshine.
F/16	Bright sea and sky subjects.

It must be understood that the foregoing are not set down as hard and fast guiding rules, but they may be safely taken as some indication of what should be done under such varying conditions. They may be said to apply generally to the temperate zones where the conditions are almost identical, irrespective of geographical situation. If the beginner follows them at first he will not make very serious mistakes. But, as has been said, experience alone can finally determine the factor of lens aperture.

The size of the aperture has another far-reaching effect. This is in regard to focussing. With the 2-inch Zeiss-Tessar lens of the William-son camera when the largest aperture is used, nothing important in the picture should be within a distance of 20 feet. If it is, it will not be in focus. As the diaphragm is closed this distance decreases proportionately until the infinity, INF, mark is reached. At this point practically everything is in focus. The distance when other objects are in focus at the respective stops is as follows.

$f/3.5$	focus distance		20 feet
$f/4$	„	„	20 „
$f/5.6$	„	„	15 „
$f/8$	„	„	12 „
$f/11$	„	„	10 „
$f/16$	„	„	5 „
INF	„	„	everything.

At first sight the fact that the camera is operated by the turning of a handle makes it seem to be absurdly simple. One or two experiments however, will prove that it is far from being as easy as it looks. The salient point is to turn the handle steadily and evenly so as to complete two revolutions per second. The first pictures will be found to be very unsatisfactory, having an eccentric jerky effect instead of a smooth easy animation. An even pressure must be maintained throughout the complete rotation, and, before the beginner attempts to take any pictures and thereby waste expensive film, he would do well to practise handle-turning until he has become proficient. If the turning movement is timed with a watch, and "one" corresponding to a second is counted for each double turn, a perfectly steady turning movement will soon be attained. Some cameras are fitted with an indicator which records the number of feet of film consumed. But no anxiety need be felt if this convenience is absent. The operator need only count one, two, three, and so on, while turning the handle, each number representing a double turn. In this way, as 16 pictures, equivalent to one foot of film, are made with every double turn and every one count, the number reached at the end of the task will show how many feet of ribbon have been used, and if this is deducted from the amount originally held by the loaded box it is easy to tell the length of film unused. When the upper box has been exhausted and the lower box filled, the latter is withdrawn and packed away to be opened in the dark room only. The empty upper box is taken out and slipped into the lower position to act as a receiver from the next loaded film-box.

In photographing, the operator must keep his eyes riveted upon the view finder, to make sure that the subject he desires is in the field of the lens. The movements can be followed easily, and there should be no difficulty in keeping the most important part of the subject in the centre of the picture.

To follow the subject either in a horizontal or vertical plane it is necessary to turn the handle controlling the panoramic movements of the tripod head. This mechanism should be turned slowly and steadily with one hand, while the other is turning the camera handle. It is by no means an easy, simple matter to follow a subject in this way without any disconcerting jerky movement, since it involves doing two things at once. For a beginner it is particularly exacting, as an eye must be kept fixed upon the view finder to follow the moving object. But after a little experience the whole of these movements are carried out in a semi-mechanical manner. In cinematography, it is the diligent, careful, and persevering worker who scores successes. In the beginning failures may be galling and frequent, but practice and experience are the best teachers. One can soon become adept in a fascinating art.

CHAPTER V

During the past few years competition among professional moving-picture photographers has become exceedingly keen, especially in connection with the filming of topical events. The operator often is faced with prodigious obstacles, the subjugation of which is not always easy, or even possible. For instance, in a dense crowd the conventional apparatus, from its bulkiness, weight, and proportions, cannot be handled, and, even if set upon its tripod with the lens elevated above the heads of the people, there is the serious danger of the whole being upset by the swaying motion of the mass of spectators. Yet at the same time a place in the crowd constitutes an ideal point of view.

Again, there are many situations where the use of a tripod is impracticable, if not dangerous. Take the aeroplane. An operator seated in a flying machine and desirous of recording the moving scenes beneath, cannot support his machine upon the conventional device for this purpose. He has to hold it as best he can, and

E 2

so secure his pictures under extremely trying conditions. Although films innumerable are taken by persons seated in aeroplanes, only a very small proportion ever come before the public eye, for the majority are failures. Nowadays, also, the filming of aeroplane flights from a fixed point on the ground is by no means easy. In order to follow the evolutions of flying machines, more particularly at comparatively close ranges and when travelling at high speeds, two operators are required, one to turn the camera handle, and the other to sight and follow the object both through its horizontal and vertical planes in such a way as to keep it in the centre of the picture. To do this he has simultaneously to turn the two handles operating the panoramic and elevating gear of the tripod head, and often in opposite directions. The task must be done without the slightest jerk, or the success of the film is marred. One of the most disconcerting effects upon the screen is a jumpy panoramic movement either horizontally or up and down. It worries the eye, and more often than not reduces the picture to an almost unintelligible blur.

But perhaps the most unnerving and difficult conditions under which moving-pictures can be taken are those pertaining to the filming of wild animal life at close range under natural con-

THE "AEROSCOPE" MOVING-PICTURE HAND CAMERA.

A. Air valve. B. Button for varying photographing speed during exposure.
C. Exposure button.

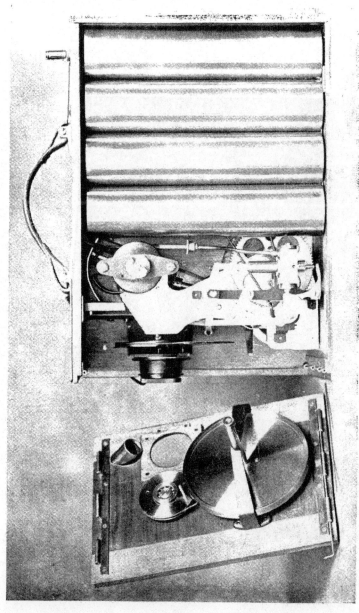

The Compressed Air Reservoirs of the "Aeroscope" Camera.
One charge is sufficient to expose 600 feet of film.

ditions. In this case a good nerve, a steady hand, and acute presence of mind, are indispensable. A wild elephant trumpetting madly and dashing towards the camera at full speed, or a lion springing towards the operator may form the subject for a thrilling incident in a film, but does not inspire confidence in the cinematographer. Under such conditions a tripod outfit is worse than useless. It not only endangers the operator's life, but the pictures taken under such conditions are invariably of poor quality, even if they survive the results of the animal's mad frenzy. To stand one's ground and to keep turning the camera handle steadily at two revolutions per second up to the last moment with the *sang-froid* of someone filming a street procession would put too great a strain on human nature. Even the coolest man would not obtain first-class results at uncomfortably close quarters. Instead of turning the handle in a steady rhythmic manner the motion would be in a series of erratic jerks, some fast and some slow, producing a result which the public would ridicule. Mr. Cherry Kearton, whose pictures of jungle life constitute some of the marvels of the cinematographic art, considers that this branch of cinematography cannot be excelled for thrilling excitement. The operator must stand his ground undismayed, because the close-quarter pictures

are always the most fascinating. Yet at the same
time he must keep a corner of one eye fixed upon
an avenue of retreat, so that he can get clear in
the nick of time when the crisis arises. The
attention given to the photographic work must
be reduced to the absolute minimum, so as to
be practically automatic ; the camera must be as
small and as compact as possible, for the only
way of escape lies often up a tree.

Several inventors have devoted their energies
to the evolution of a reliable hand-camera, capable
of fulfilling the same duty in cinematography as
the snap-shot instrument in still-life work. The
tripod was sacrificed, but then there arose another
difficulty. This was in the necessity of moving
the film mechanism by means of the handle. In
fact, under many conditions of working, such as
in the jungle, it would be quite impracticable.
What was required was an efficient moving-picture
machine, small, light, and compact, working upon
the principle of " you-press-the-button-and-I'll-do-
the-rest."

It is a perplexing problem to solve, and the
first commercially practicable idea in this direction
was conceived by the Polish scientist Kasimir de
Proszynski. He has produced a camera completely self-contained and wholly automatic in its
operation. Dimensions and weight have been
kept down. In loaded condition, with 300 feet

of film, it is 12 inches long, 8½ inches wide, 6½ inches deep, and weighs only 14 pounds. It works upon the " press-the-button " system, the film-moving mechanism and shutter running the whole time the button is depressed. The power comes from cylinders of compressed air by which a tiny engine is driven. All that the operator has to do is to sight his subject and to keep his finger on the button, while he follows the object on the view finder.

When this camera, known as the "aeroscope," appeared upon the market, it aroused consider-able interest, but its reliability was doubted. It was not until Mr. Cherry Kearton decided to give it a trial that it came to be regarded more seriously as a feasible moving-picture machine. This naturalist-cinematographer took it with him on one of his expeditions, and was able to record some startling incidents which would not have been possible otherwise. Familiarity with the camera and experience in the field convinced him of its serviceability, provided that certain modifications were effected. These were carried out, and the camera is now regarded as an excel-lent instrument for work that could not be achieved by any other machine.

It is fitted, as has been said, with a small engine driven by compressed air. The air is stored in six small cylinders of an aggregate capacity of

600 feet. This is sufficient to expose 600 feet of film. The cylinders are charged with air in the manner of a motor tyre and with a similar kind of pump. An indicator on the side shows constantly the air pressure remaining in the reservoirs, while a regulator enables the speed to be varied. The driving mechanism is very light, small, and compact, and contains but a small number of parts, so that the risk of failure is not great. Though it constitutes the most delicate part of the whole mechanism, and requires careful handling, it works remarkably well so long as it is kept clean and well lubricated.

Another prominent feature of the mechanism is what is termed an equilibrator. Practically speaking this is a small gyroscope, and is introduced to subdue any small vibrations or tremblings which arise while the instrument is working. This part of the mechanism has been criticized on the ground that a gyroscope, to be effective, must be of appreciable weight. Many operators dispute the necessity for its introduction. They point out that the beneficial effects are not proportionate to the extra weight involved. Furthermore, being an additional piece of mechanism, it enhances the risk of derangement. Against these contentions, however, the operators who have worked the instrument maintain that it nullifies all the

THE LENS, SHUTTER, COMPRESSED AIR-DRIVEN MECHANISM, AND GYROSCOPE, WHICH COUNTERACTS SLIGHT VIBRA-TIONS, OF THE " AEROSCOPE."

LOADING THE "AEROSCOPE" CAMERA.
The unexposed and exposed film-boxes are mounted upon one spindle.

vibrations set up by the driving mechanism, which, though apparently slight, would otherwise suffice to spoil the pictures. Seeing that the sole object of employing this camera is the elimination of a rigid support such as a tripod, it certainly seems worth while, even at the cost of added weight, to gain some compensating steadiness. And the vibration of the air engine increases the need.

In operating this instrument the usual method is to hold the camera against the chest and one cheek, thereby bringing the eye on a level with the sighting piece. By letting the elbows rest against the body the weight is easily and steadily supported. Held in this position the minimum of fatigue is felt by the cinematographer, while he is given complete control over the mechanism. It can also be used when the operator is on horseback, the method of support being virtually the same. But in this case only one hand is used; the other is left free to control the horse. Another advantage of the system is the ease with which the camera can be swung round in order to follow a moving object steadily.

Photographers who use a hand-camera are familiar with the disturbances set up by the motion of the body in breathing. This is often sufficient to spoil a picture if care is not displayed at the instant of exposure. With the aeroscope—

owing to the exposure being from $\frac{1}{32}$ to $\frac{1}{50}$ of a second, relatively long in comparison with snap-shotting where the exposure is often only the $\frac{1}{200}$, or even less, of a second—these disturbances are somewhat more acute. Considerable practice is required before this difficulty can be overcome. Some operators who have used the aeroscope prefer to utilise a convenient support, if available, such as a wall, or the stump of a tree, thereby making sure of a solid rigid foundation. But in cinematography the ill-effects arising from respiration are not so serious as in still-life work. A picture here and there may show its effects, but they pass unnoticed. They are subdued, as it were, by the unblemished pictures which precede and follow.

Another camera of this type is the "Jury Autocam" which, as its name implies, works upon the automatic "press-the-button" system. This camera is fitted with a small electric motor, driven by a small dry battery, and brought into action by the pressure of a button. A small side-lever controls the picture-taking speed, which can be varied while the mechanism is running. The camera itself is exactly similar to the "Jury Duplex" model, the only addition being a small separate case, about 2 inches in depth, fitted to the base of the instrument, and a covered chain gearing on one side for transmitting the power

Mr. Cherry Kearton slung over a cliff, showing the operation of the hand camera.

Mr. Cherry Kearton steadying himself upon
a precipice to take pictures of bird life.

THE "AEROSCOPE" CAMERA IN THE FIELD.

From the " Cinema College," by permission of the   *Motograph Co.*

VULTURE PREPARING TO FLY.

from the motor to the camera mechanism. This camera likewise is fitted with a small balancing apparatus to counteract slight vibrations.

In such instruments as these the even running of the motor is a vital factor. It must not run any faster when the reservoir or battery is fully charged than when it is nearly exhausted, nor must there be any variations of speed, for eccentricities of this sort are apt to spoil the film. The governing therefore requires to be most delicate and thorough. Another difficulty is the incorporation of a reservoir capable of carrying a sufficient quantity of air at the necessary pressure to drive the length of film for which it is rated. In the "Jury Autocam" a length of 100 feet can be driven on a single battery charge. This is adequate for many purposes, but a length of at least 200 feet is generally to be preferred. The camera is being adapted to meet these conditions, and it is anticipated that no more difficulty will be met in consummating this end, than was involved in making the camera drive a 100 feet length.

While it is a moot point whether the automatic cinematograph camera will ever displace the orthodox machine entirely, it is a useful and even indispensable machine for working under difficulties. It has been used in the aeroplane and has been found successful. It is also of the utmost use in close-range dangerous work, or in situations where the turning of the handle by hand is liable to be carried out imperfectly and unsteadily. The aeroscope camera has been used on many notable expeditions such as those of Paul Rainey, and others in Africa, and is used exclusively by Mr. Cherry Kearton in his daring work in tight corners. Many of the thrilling and exciting pictures taken in the haunts of wild animals have been secured therewith, and these films show convincingly what can be done with the instrument when it is handled by an expert.

But the true province of the hand cinematograph camera undoubtedly is in connection with rush work. For the filming of topical incidents it is invaluable. The operator is not tramelled with a bulky outfit. He carries his camera in his hand or slings it across his back in the manner of a knap-sack. When he wishes to film an incident he is not harassed even by the crowd. He is not compelled to set up a tripod or to climb to an elevated point to get clear of the sea of heads. He can hold the camera above his head, and by means of a second and special view finder placed on the under side of the instrument he can sight and follow the subject while pressing the button. Thus he records the episode as easily as if he were placed in the most advantageous raised position, and could manipulate the machine in the orthodox manner. When his work is completed he can get away without any delay, because the small box contains everything.

On the whole, however, the hand moving-picture camera is scarcely yet a suitable instrument for beginners. The invention is in its infancy, and although clever men are striving to make it more simple and reliable, many peculiar problems still remain to be solved. But in the hands of an expert operator it is capable of doing first-class work.

CHAPTER VI

DEVELOPING THE FILM

THE beginner, when he handles for the first time a coil of sensitized film measuring $1\frac{3}{8}$ inches in width, and perhaps 200 feet in length, might hesitate to attempt its development. He might prefer to despatch it to a firm prepared to carry out this work for a light charge, confident that with the facilities at their command, and with their accumulated experience, they would be able to bring out his work to the best advantage.

But the man who aspires to succeed in topical work for the local picture palace or general market, especially if he is not within easy reach of a post office, must be prepared to undertake the task himself. As a matter of fact it is by no means so difficult as it appears at first sight, and the rudiments of the process may be grasped readily by a person of average intelligence. Success, as in other handicrafts, only can be achieved with practice.

Cinematography, being a peculiar and special branch of the photographic art, demanding the

use of new and unfamiliar tools, has been responsible for the perfection of particular devices and
methods to assist and facilitate development.   In
the early days the worker had to worry through
the task, and was compelled to undertake a host
of doubtful experiments.   The beginner of to-day
is able to profit from the mistakes of the pioneers,
and the appliances and processes at his disposal
are those of approved application.   After one or
two trials the worker will realise that the development of a 200-feet length of celluloid ribbon is
no more difficult than the development of an
ordinary Kodak spool.

One thing the beginner will do well to bear in
mind.   He should adopt some particular brand
of film, and cling to it after he has become
acquainted with its emulsion, speed, composition,
and peculiar characteristics.   There are three or
four different makes of film upon the market, but
it is preferable to select a film which is easily
obtainable at any time and in any part of the
world.   I would strongly urge the beginner to
select the Eastman stock for this if for no other
reason.   The Eastman organisation has its ten-
tacles spread throughout the world.   It has
thousands of agencies in immediate touch with
the different national companies.   The result is
that this film can be purchased without difficulty
in nearly all parts of the globe.   If a local dealer

does not stock it, he can procure it to order within a day or two.   Moreover the film will be new and in perfect condition.

There are many other reasons why it is advisable to select and to adhere to this stock, which, although of a technical character, are of much importance to the user.   It must be borne in mind that the technics and chemistry of cinematography are still in their infancy, and the technical staff retained for the preparation of the various ingredients employed in the sensitizing of the film are striving constantly to improve and to increase the speed or sensitiveness of the emulsion.   The result is that the worker who uses Eastman film keeps pace with developments.   The makers of this ribbon were the first to discover a base and emulsion suited to moving-picture work.   This was achieved only after the expenditure of enormous sums of money, after hundreds of fruitless experiments, and with the co-operation of the highest technical and chemical skill.   Under these circumstances the limitations of the base and of the emulsion become thoroughly understood, so that the film is certain to maintain the highest quality.   On the other hand, those firms who have embarked upon the manufacture of the commodity only within recent years, have still to face and to overcome many pitfalls which the older concern discovered and surmounted years ago.   So the

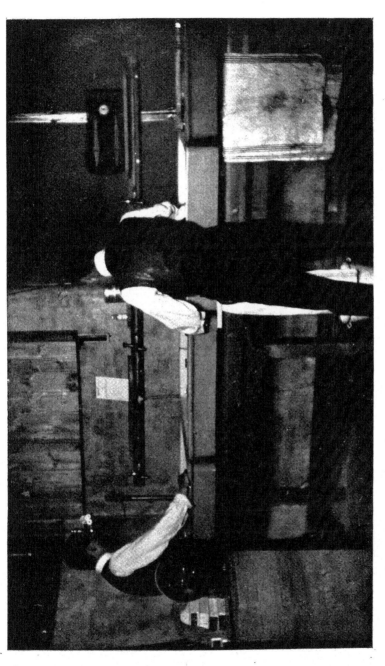

A WELL-EQUIPPED DARK ROOM SHOWING ARRANGEMENT OF THE TRAYS.

By permission of   *Jury's Kine. Supplies, Ltd.*

WINDING THE DEVELOPING FRAME.

The film is transferred from the exposed film-box to a revolving frame, emulsion side outermost.

film marketed by younger organisations is apt to vary in its quality.

Before the beginner attempts development he must make sure that his dark room and accessories are adequate. To seek success with makeshifts in the first instance is to court heart-rending failure. Many of the utensils employed in the dark room can be fashioned by any handy man. They may lack finish, but so long as they perform their work properly nothing more is necessary.

The dark room must be spacious, for cramped conditions are fatal to satisfactory work. An expert will perform his task successfully, if the exigencies arise, in a small cupboard, but the beginner will find that the more space he has at his command the easier he will be able to complete his task. The room should measure 10 feet in length by 6 feet wide at least. In a corner, or at some other convenient point along the wall, there should be an ordinary sink provided with free waste and with ample supplies of water laid on to a tap above. On one or other side of this sink, there should be a bench, 3 feet in width, for the purpose of the developing, fixing, rinsing, and other baths.

At least four trays will be required, three being for solutions and one for rinsing. Each tray should be at least 33 inches square inside, by about 6 inches in depth. These trays may be made of wood throughout, with dove-tailed sides, and tongued and grooved bottom, or the bottom may be made of glass. If the work of dove-tailing seems too difficult, the sides and bottom need only be nailed or screwed together, but in this case a lining of waterproof fabric should be fixed to the wood. Trays of this type are inexpensive, and are quite as good as those of a more elaborate character. In some developing works lead-lined trays are used, but they are weighty and cumbersome to handle. In order to draw off the solution when necessary it is well to fit a drain and plug in the bottom of the tray by which the contents can escape into the storage vessel placed beneath the bench.

Sometimes a vertical tank is used. This system is maintained to be the most satisfactory as it enables the solution to be kept more easily in movement. The tank, in this case, should be 33 inches high by 33 inches wide, and 6 inches from front to back. These are inside measurements. It must be lined with waterproof material or with thin sheet lead in the same manner as the tray. For the purposes of the small worker, the tank process is more expensive, owing to the greater quantity of solution that it requires; so, for ordinary and limited working, the tray is recommended. It should be fitted with a rocker so as to enable the solution to be kept flowing evenly over the surface of the film.

The film is mounted upon a special frame. A frame made of wood is most generally used. This likewise a handy man can make at home, although it is not expensive to buy. The middle of each side of the frame is fitted with a short pin to

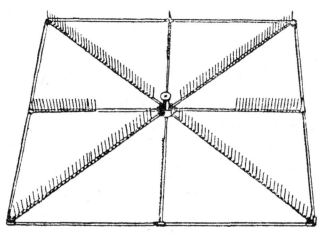

FIG. 2.—The " Pin " Frame.

serve as a spindle and to facilitate spinning round when the frame is mounted upon its stand. Each transverse end is provided with guide pins for winding the film.

The other type is known as the pin frame. Its design may be gathered from Fig. 2. It is a light skeleton frame with vertical pins projecting from the four diagonal members. The spool is slipped on the central spindle and the film is unwound and passed round the pin on one diagonal, then to the relative pins on the three other members. It is then taken round the second pin on the first diagonal, followed round the relative pins on the other three members, and so on until the whole film has been uncoiled, the pins on the other four cross members being called into requisition as additional supports when the frame is about half covered. When the film is mounted upon this frame it is in the form of an endless square spiral. When the frame is laid in the bath of solution the film stands edgewise. The wooden frame, however, is now almost exclusively used, as it is easier and simpler to work. The film can be transferred to it in a shorter space of time, and the frame with the film upon it can be handled more safely.

The ruby light may be either electricity, gas, or oil, but extreme care must be taken to make absolutely certain that the light is non-actinic, and is not too powerful, otherwise the film, which is extremely sensitive, will be fogged during development. The safety of the light may be tested in a very simple and easy manner. Cut off about 6 inches of film from the unexposed reel, lay it flat upon the developing bench, emulsion side uppermost, in full view of the ruby light. Place two or three coins upon the emulsion and leave them there for a few minutes. Then develop the strip in a covered dish. If the space surrounding the places where the coins were laid comes up grey, then it shows that the light is unsafe, because the exposed emulsion surrounding the coins has become fogged. On the other hand, if no signs of the position of the coins are revealed upon the developed strip, the light is perfectly safe.

The trays should be placed side by side along the bench. The one which is used for developing should stand furthest from the ruby light. If space will allow, the rinsing bath should be placed next to it, but if this is impossible the fixing bath may be placed there. A division board should be set up between the two trays, rising some 10 or 12 inches above their upper edges. This will prevent the fixing solution splashing into the developing bath and spoiling it. Various formulæ have been prepared for development, each of which has certain advantages. As may be supposed, each firm has evolved a formula which it has found from experience to give the best results. Obviously these formulæ are secret. But the most satisfactory for the beginner is that advocated by the Eastman Company. It possesses the advantage of having been prepared by the chemists who are responsible for the emulsion, who understand its particular characteristics and also its limita-

tions. The majority of other formulæ are based
more or less upon this one, which is applicable
and adaptable to all kinds of work. It has the
quality of bringing the picture out to the utmost
degree, and by its means many of the errors in
exposure may be corrected during development.
The developing solution is made up as
follows :—

	Avoirdupois.	Metric.
Sodium sulphite (des.) ...	53 oz.	1,575 grammes
Sodium carbonate („) ...	25 ,,	750 ,,
Metol	180 grains	12 ,,
Hydrochinon (hydroquinone)	8 oz.	237 ,,
Potassium bromide	1 oz. 63 grains	34 ,,
Citric acid	400 grains	27·5 ,,
Potassium metabisulphite ...	2 oz.	60 ,,
Water (Imperial measure) ⎱	8¼ gallons	
„ (United States „ ⎰	10 ,,	40 litres

The ingredients must be mixed in the order
indicated. All the chemicals are readily and
cheaply obtainable at any photographic chemists
and drug stores. After preparation the developer
will keep for a long period so long as the
bottle is well stoppered and kept in a cool place.
Only the highest grade chemicals of a reputable
brand should be used. A slight saving in the
purchase of these essentials is false economy,
because a film costing one hundred or more

times the money saved in the outlay upon chemicals may thus be ruined.

In cases of over-exposure, perhaps the most common fault of the beginner who does not understand the stopping down of the lens, a restrainer is necessary. This is composed of the following :—

	Avoirdupois.	Metric.
Potassium bromide	1 oz.	30 grammes
Water	10 oz.	300 cubic centimetres

The process of development is as follows. First, the film is transferred from the dark film-box of the camera to the frame. The latter, if it is of the wooden type, can be spun round freely when mounted on its stand. It is not advisable for the beginner to withdraw the coil of film bodily from the box until he is expert in winding the frame, otherwise, to his surprise and disgust, the spool may fall out and the film be precipitated to the floor in an inextricable tangle. He should let it remain in the dark box until it is removed by being drawn slowly through the velvet-lined slot. The free end of the film should be fixed with a drawing pin to one end-bar of the frame, and contained between two guide pins, with the emulsion side outermost. The emulsion side

can be recognized even in the subdued light of
the dark room because it has a matt surface, while
the other side is glossy. The difference between
the two sides can also be detected by the touch.
When the end of the film has been attached to
one end-bar the frame is turned, the film mean-
while being permitted to slide out of the dark
box, until the opposite end of the frame comes
up. The film is passed over this bar, also
between the first pair of guide pins, and once
more, with a half-turn to the frame, the film
passes along the second side of the frame back
to the first bar, between the succeeding pair of
guide pins, over the top and back again to the
opposite bar, this process being continued until
the coil of film is unrolled, when the second
extremity is likewise fixed to the bar by means
of a drawing pin. The film while being wound
must not be drawn too tightly ; at the same time
it must not be too slack. When winding has
been completed, the frame and film will have the
appearance shown in the illustration facing p. 65.
The guide pins in the end bars prevent the edges
from overlapping or touching. The result is the
presentation of two emulsion faces on either side
of the frame and each face resembles the sensitized
side of a dry plate.

In winding the film upon the frame, and indeed
during all the operations, the operator should be

The FILM TRANSFERRED FROM THE DEVELOPING FRAME TO THE DRYING DRUM.

For amateur use a small drum can be used.

By permission of   Williamson Kine. Co., Ltd.

THE FILM WOUND ON FRAME AND PLACED IN
THE DEVELOPING TRAY.

By permission of   Jury's Kine. Supplies, Ltd.

THE JURY COMBINED CAMERA AND PRINTER,

careful not to touch the gelatine coating of the ribbon with his fingers. The finger nails should be kept well trimmed so that scratching may be avoided. A touched film is usually marked, for the touch leaves a deposit of grease, which interferes with the action of the developer.

The frame, with the film wound upon it, is lifted off the stand and carefully placed in the developing bath, into which the developing solution has already been poured. If it is inserted gently no air bubbles or bells will form on the emulsion, but if there should be any such they can be removed at once by means of a large, flat, soft, camel hair brush. In order to secure first-class results, the developing solution should be kept at a temperature of 65° Fahr.

The developing solution is rapid in its action and the film must be watched closely. The frame must be kept rocking so that the solution may remain in movement. This enables it to act upon the whole surface of the film equally. Should development take place too quickly— (*i.e.* the images flash up almost instantly)—the frame should be removed at once from the developer and immersed in the rinsing tray to allow a few drams of the restrainer solution to be poured into, and mixed with, the developer. On the other hand the film may be under-exposed, and then the images will appear very slowly.

Development proceeds exactly as in the case of a glass plate, and the same judgment is required to determine when the process has been carried far enough.   When this point has been reached the frame is lifted out of the developer and placed in the rinsing tray to receive a thorough washing. Water is a kind friend in cinematography and should be used ungrudgingly. Three or four thorough flushes will suffice to rinse the film satisfactorily, and then the frame is placed in the fixing bath.   This is made up as follows :—

	Avoirdupois.	Metric.
Water	64 oz. (fluid)	2,000 c.c.
Hyposulphite of soda	16 ,,	480 grammes
Sulphite	¾ ,,	22 ,,

When fully dissolved add the following hardener.

	Avoirdupois.	Metric.
Powdered alum ...	½ oz.	15 grammes
Citric acid	½ ,,	15 ,,

During fixing the frame should be kept rocked so that every trace of undeveloped silver salts may be removed from the film. Then it is transferred to the washing tray and submitted to a thorough washing in frequent changes of water for some twenty minutes. The film is now ready for its final treatment. This is immersion in the soaking solution :—

	Avoirdupois.	Metric.
Water...	32 oz.	1,000 c.c.
Glycerine	1 „	30 „

This final bath is not always used, but it is desirable if the negative film is to be kept for any length of time. Immersion in this soaking solution prevents the gelatine coating of the film from becoming hard and horny. After remaining in this bath for five minutes the frame is lifted out, and returned to its stand, where the excess of glycerine and water is removed by wiping with a soft cloth.

It will be seen that once the film is wound upon the frame it is not removed during the whole process of development, and may be left in the same position during the drying period. But if the drying is to be quickly performed the frame must be of what is known as the spring type, so that it does not keep the same area of film constantly pressing upon the curved end-bars. Otherwise the film would retain this shape when it has been dried and the kink would be irremovable. To avoid this defect it is just as well to transfer the film from the frame to a drum (see illustration facing p. 72). This is an easy matter. The drum is mounted upon a stand so as to be free to revolve easily. Detach one end of the film from the developing frame, and attach it to the drum by means of a drawing pin. The emulsion side, of course, must face outwards. Then by unwinding the frame and rotating the drum simultaneously the film becomes wound spirally upon the drum. Another pin will secure the second end of the film. The drum is an inexpensive and very handy accessory to the moving-picture photographer, especially in the drying operation, when forceful methods have to be adopted.

Unfortunately the drying of the film cannot be accelerated to any great extent. The hardening of the gelatine emulsion cannot be hastened, as in glass plate work, by immersion in a bath of methylated spirits or some other evaporative agent, since the alcohol contained therein would dissolve the celluloid base. The only available means is a current of warm, dry, clean air. While the well-equipped factory is fitted with a special drying room, such a facility is beyond the resources of the average independent worker, who must therefore be content to revolve his frame or drum continuously, until the gelatine has hardened sufficiently The process can be accelerated to a certain extent by revolving the drum or frame over a steam radiator, or some other form of heating which emits no smoke or flame, but the temperature of the air must not be raised too high or the gelatine coating will be injured. If the weather is fine and calm, the drying may be done upon a lawn in the open air, but in any event extreme care must be observed to prevent dust settling upon the gelatine while it is wet and soft, or irreparable injury will be inflicted. So it behoves the worker to keep his dark room and drying room free from dust. Drying should not be done in the dark room because there are small particles of chemical dust always floating about in such surroundings. If these should settle upon the emulsion they would play sad havoc with it.

When the gelatine has hardened the film may be transferred direct from the drum to a spool by means of a winder. When the beginner has become expert he will be able to do this by hand, but it is never a wise practice since the coating is liable to become scratched. The spool-winder is inexpensive and does the work much more quickly, while the risk of damaging the film is eliminated.

As has been mentioned, it is well to develop

the film as soon as possible after exposure. Although the exposed film is kept in a dark box, the chemical action set up by exposure before the lens, continues, as in dry-plate and snap-shot photography, and in a more rapid manner. Consequently the film should not be left undeveloped for more than a few days at the utmost. While prompt development is usual in topical work, there are other sorts of work in which the operator may feel tempted to put the film on one side for development at a later and more convenient time. Perhaps several weeks may elapse, and then complete amazement is expressed at the result. In the unexposed condition, however, Eastman stock will last many months so long as it is not removed from the case in which it is packed at the works. Equal care must be used in storing the developed negative films. They must be kept in a cool dry place, protected from severe fluctuations in temperature and climatic effects.

CHAPTER VII

PRINTING THE POSITIVE

THEORETICALLY there is no operation in the whole art of cinematography which is more complex than the preparation of the positive. This is used for projecting the image on the screen, and is the result upon which popular criticism is passed. Also, in the process of printing the positive, several short-comings in the negative can be corrected.

At the same time, from the practical point of view, the preparation of the positive is simple. The beginner who has mastered the somewhat intricate process of development, need not apprehend any greater difficulties than those he has already overcome before he essays to print his positive. In practice he will soon become proficient, though he may retain rather hazy ideas of the theory of the matter.

The essentials for the preparation of the positive are a printing machine and an illuminant. The appliances and methods of operation differ completely from those used in any other branch of photography, so that a new art virtually has to be mastered. Fortunately, the beginner gets assistance from those masters of the craft, who, having left the producing for the manufacturing side of the industry, willingly give advice to the tyro. By following the few rules which these early workers lay down, the beginner will not go far wrong, and will not run the risk of incurring many dispiriting failures. While the large professional firms use elaborate and costly printing machines, the amateur is able to get just as good results with simpler and cheaper apparatus. He could not wish for a better equipment than the Williamson printer, which costs only £4 10s. ($22.50), or the Jury Duplex, which is a combined camera and printer.

So far as the illuminant is concerned this depends upon circumstances. In most towns it is possible to obtain electric light, which is the simplest, and taken all round, the most reliable and satisfactory illuminant. If this is not available, gas and an incandescent mantle may be used. Failing either of these conveniences, acetylene or petrol gas, the latter with the incandescent gas mantle, can take their place. Even daylight may be used.

Success in printing depends upon a correct judgment of the intensity of the light, and of the density of the film. This enables one to estimate the exposure required. Obviously this knowledge can only be acquired in the school of practice. The same experience is needed to estimate the length of the exposure in making lantern slides, or in bromide printing. But it must be borne in mind that in the cinematograph film one is working with a much more sensitive emulsion.

A very good practice for the beginner is to make experimental exposures with short lengths of film—say 12 inches—making the tests with sections of the negative which vary in density, at various distances from the light, and at different speeds. A careful note should be made of each trial. In this way one can estimate the exposure and learn how it should be varied at different points of the negative where the density varies. Moreover, the knowledge will be acquired at comparatively little expense.

If the negative has been over-exposed or over-developed, or both, a common error in the first attempts, it will naturally be very dense, and will demand a longer exposure, or a more powerful light, than a negative which is exposed correctly. This situation may be met either by slowing down the process of printing, or by bringing the light nearer to the film. On the other hand, if a negative is under-exposed it had better be destroyed at once, as it is worse than useless. An over-exposed negative will yield a passable print, possibly somewhat harsh, but nothing can be done with a negative which is deficient in detail. The only exception that may be made to this drastic policy is the topical film, which may have been taken under adverse conditions, during a fog, or in heavy rain, or on a dull day, or at a late hour when the light was bad. In the topical film it is more the interest of the event than the quality of the film that is important.

For absolute simplicity it would be difficult to excel the system adopted in the Jury Duplex camera. In this case one obtains both camera and printing apparatus—without the lens—for the modest outlay of £8 ($40). There is a small bracket mounted upon the outer top face, and near the front edge, of the case. This bracket carries the spool on which the negative film is coiled. This is slipped on the bobbin and locked in position by means of a small lever. The film is carried from this spool between two small guide pressure rollers and fed into the camera through a slot faced with velvet, like that provided in the dark boxes. The film is pulled down a sufficient distance to enter the gate so as to secure engagement by the claws of the camera mechanism. In threading the film care must be used to bring the emulsion side facing the dark boxes and the glossy side facing the lens.

The positive film is inserted in the unexposed film-box of the camera and is threaded up as if for taking photographs.   As the emulsion side is uppermost, when the unexposed film meets the negative in the gate, the two films are brought together with their emulsion sides in contact. As one film is laid squarely over the other, and with the perforations in line, it will be seen that the claws engage with both, so that the two films are jerked together intermittently through the gate.

Emerging from the gate the two films part company. The exposed positive ribbon passes into the exposed dark box, while the negative film passes through another velvet-lined slot in the bottom of the camera, and then is wound up on another spool.

It will be seen that in this case printing is carried out in a manner similar to photographing. The film is run through the camera in the ordinary way by turning the handle, and the number of exposures per second can be varied within wide limits to suit the density of the film. The camera is supplied with a second spindle and gearing upon which the handle may be slipped. The ratio of this gearing is one exposure per revolution, or as it is termed "one turn per picture."

Owing to the positive film being contained within the camera, and therefore in a light-tight space, the electric light or other illuminant may be mounted upon the bench within the dark room, so that the operator can work in a lighted apartment. In this arrangement, however, the camera should be clamped firmly to a rigid foundation, so that it may not move during exposure. This also ensures that the light should remain at a constant distance from the machine.

This camera can be adjusted easily and cheaply for the purpose of daylight printing. All that is required is a square funnel, about two feet in length, made of wood and so designed that the smaller open end fits into the front recess of the camera after the shutter panel is removed or opened. This funnel should be made after the manner of a Kodak enlarger, and blackened on the inside, with a dull medium, so that no reflections of light are set up. When this funnel is attached it is only necessary to stand the camera on its rear face so that the opening of the funnel points directly to the clear sky overhead, not towards the sun, and to turn the handle upon the one turn one picture gear. The printing speed will vary with the intensity of the light and the density of the film. Obviously the camera can be run more rapidly on a bright summer than on a dull winter day. In the first case it is safe to turn the handle as fast as possible, but in the second the speed would need to be about one picture, or handle turn, per second.

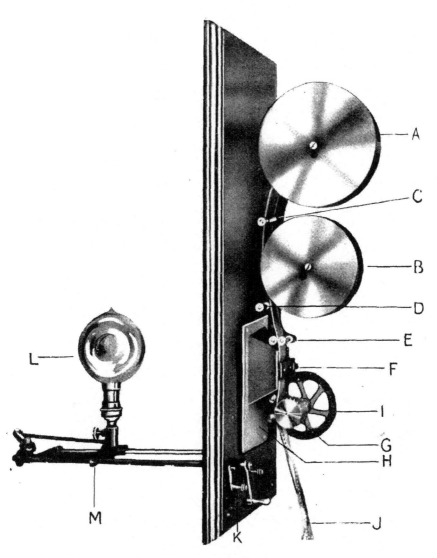

THE WILLIAMSON PRINTER.

(For explanation see p. 85.)

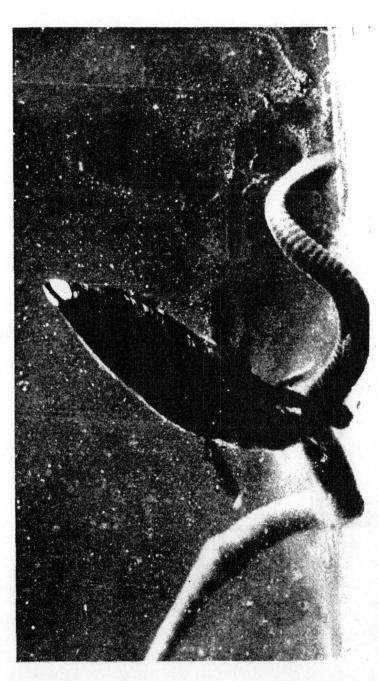

Motograph Co.

From the "Cinema College," by permission of the

WATER BEETLE ATTACKING A WORM.

One advantage of this system of printing is that the picture is printed with the camera with which the negative was obtained, and so first-class results are inevitable. The registration is assured as well as the alignment. In threading up the camera it is only necessary to make sure that the image on the negative comes squarely and truly before the window in the gate. Once this is so, every successive picture must be in perfect registration and alignment. There could be no method of printing more suitable for those who are travelling, or engaged on topical work, often under trying conditions, for the conversion from photographing to printing, and *vice versâ*, may be accomplished in an instant. Some of the more expensive cameras costing from £20 ($100) upwards are now fitted with a printing attachment, the printing accessory being detached when the instrument is being used for photographing purposes. These cameras follow where the Jury Duplex led the way.

The Williamson printer works upon a different principle, being a distinct and separate machine. Nevertheless it is an eminently practical appliance, and is as well adapted to the factory as to the amateur's dark room. It comprises a base board on which the whole of the mechanism is mounted, together with the stand for the light. (See illustration facing page 84.)

In this installation there must either be a dark box to contain the light, against the face of which the base board of the printing mechanism is screwed, or else an aperture must be provided in the wall of the dark room and the light be placed on a shelf outside. The handy man, however, will be able to devise a light-tight box, either for the electric light or gas. In the latter case it must be fitted with a chimney with baffle plates absolutely light-tight, to carry off the products of combustion. The light-tight box should be lined either with absolutely safe ruby fabric, or with orange and ruby fabrics superimposed. If wood is used, the light-box is apt to split under the influence of the heat within.

The Williamson printer is of the simplest design conceivable. There is an upper spindle A (see illustration facing p. 84) on which the spool containing the negative is carried. Immediately below is another spindle carrying the spool B on which is slipped the coil of unexposed film. The negative film, emulsion side outermost, as it winds off the spool A is passed behind the guide roller C and then picks up the unexposed film of spool B. The emulsion side of the unexposed film comes into contact with the emulsion side of the negative film. Passing over another guide roller D the films pass together between the two rollers E to enter the gate F. The latter is mounted upon the rear face of a small chamber, the aperture of which is of the size of the cinematograph film image. This aperture is provided on the inside with a small hinged shutter. By opening this one can see that the negative image occupies the full space of the window, or make any other observations. The film is moved intermittently through the printing gate F by the sprocket wheel G, the teeth of which engage with the perforations in the films. The engagement of the films with this sprocket is ensured by the two pressure rollers H. The sprocket G is mounted upon and revolved by the handwheel I—a motor drive can be incorporated if desired—and after being moved beyond this sprocket wheel, the two films divide, the positive film being wound upon a spool or into its dark box, while the negative is wound upon another spool. The movement of the light K, either towards or from the exposure window F, is effected by means of the handle J, which has ten stops corresponding to as many different distances. The lamp moves to and fro along the support L.

It will be seen that the Williamson is a simple, straightforward machine. It is soundly constructed and works admirably. Its achievements are in every way equal to those of the complicated and more expensive model manufactured

by the same firm for professional use.[1]   So long
as the machine works reliably, and has perfect
registration and alignment, nothing more is
required. Extra refinements, and little details,
while of service to the expert, only serve to
harass the amateur.

As a matter of fact the most important duties
of a printing machine are to feed the two films
evenly and easily through the gate, and to hold
them flatly and tightly together, so as to secure
perfect contact while they are before the exposure
window. By this instrument both these duties
are perfectly performed. The sprocket G continuously revolves under the steady turning
movement of the handle, and the two films are
held rigidly, tightly and steadily together by the
pressure gate F.

Of course, in printing with this machine, the
operator works in total darkness, owing to the
coil of positive film being fully exposed. This
is no handicap however, because the dark-room
ruby lamp supplies sufficient light to enable
the necessary operations to be performed. But
it is not wise to use too powerful a ruby light,
or the unexposed positive film will be fogged.

Turning the driving handle is no more difficult
than turning that of the camera mechanism.

[1] "Moving Pictures : How they are Made and Worked,"
Chapter VIII., page 82.

The gearing is so designed that six exposures are made per revolution, representing twelve pictures per second, when revolved at the normal speed. With a negative of average density this speed is sufficient. But the period of exposure can be varied according to the speed at which the handle is turned. The turns of the handle should be steady and regular, or the pictures will be of uneven density owing to the variations in exposure.

The electric light is easily moved by means of the handle while the ten stops give it great flexibility. In order to maintain an exposure of twelve pictures per second with an average negative, a lamp of 50 candle power should be used. To ensure the best results it should be of the class known as "focus lamp." This type of lamp has a special filament, with a smaller coil than is found in the ordinary incandescent electric lamp. A gas burner with incandescent mantle may be used if electricity is not available, though the operator will have to ascertain the relative value of the luminous intensity of the light as compared with the 50 candle power electric light, and will be wise if he makes one or two trial exposures with short lengths of film before essaying the printing of a complete film.

While it is possible during printing to vary

the distance of the light from the exposure window, the light being manipulated with the left hand, while the handle is turned with the right, there is slight necessity for such a procedure. The negative film should be examined to ascertain how the density varies along its length, and then each portion of film that shows tolerable regularity of density should be printed off at the same speed. In this way variations of distance need occur only with distinct lengths of film. This is a far safer method, especially for the beginner, than the movement of the light to and fro while the films are running through the gate, though of course with practice it becomes possible to do the two things satisfactorily at once. Many amateur cinematographers make the mistake of attempting artifices which they have seen practised by some experienced professional worker, and the result is failure. What is easy and simple to the expert is often beyond the powers of the beginner. Success in printing can only be achieved by honest and diligent work, but patience is sure of its reward. At first there may be a tendency to make the positives somewhat too dense, and then, when the evils of this defect are appreciated, to fly to the opposite extreme. Of the two blemishes probably the latter is the worse, as it produces a washed-out effect upon the screen.

The positive is developed in exactly the same way as the negative, and with the same solutions. When dry the positive, which may have been printed in short distinct lengths, should be connected up with the aid of cement as described in a previous chapter. If titles have to be introduced they may be inserted wherever required, merely by severing the film at that point, and introducing the length carrying the explanation.

The preparation of the titles is a simple matter. If printed type is used, the letters cut out of white paper or cardboard are laid flat upon a level surface with a black background. The camera is then placed overhead with the lens pointing downwards upon the centre of the title space. The latter, brilliantly illuminated, is then photographed at the rate of sixteen pictures per second for a period of ten seconds or more according to requirements.

In many instances, especially in non-topical work, the operator need not necessarily incur the expense and trouble of printing a positive film. Many of the purchasers of educational and popularly scientific films will give their decision after having seen the negative passed through the projector in the manner of a positive film. So long as great care is used, this can be done without ill effects, but of course the slightest scratch or abrasion that the negative may receive in the process will be reproduced with accentuated effect upon the positive film. Even with some of the topical films a positive is not necessary. To submit the negative to the local theatre or prospective purchaser is often a good way of saving time and being first in the field. Many theatres now are being equipped with dark rooms and printing machines. A glance at the negative will enable the manager to decide whether the film is serviceable or otherwise, and if a purchase is made, the deletion of the uninteresting parts can be made before printing. Incidentally, one great advantage of this is that the film is submitted for consideration about three or four hours earlier than would be the case if the independent worker struck off his own positive, and in these days of high pressure such a saving is important. It may often be the means of forestalling a competitor. Even if it is intended to supply prints to two or three different picture palaces the negative offers a means of transacting business, because the respective establishments can give their orders, make their arrangements concerning announcements, and be able to judge fairly accurately the hour at which the film will be available for projection. In one instance an independent topical worker who had a first-class negative of a popular subject drove round from theatre to theatre with his negative and secured an order for about half-a-dozen copies. He then handed over the work of printing to a professional firm. Four hours later he delivered the positives to the respective theatres, and ultimately he sold the negative outright to the firm who completed his printing contracts for the supply of other markets at their disposal. In another instance an enterprising amateur who had an excellent negative handed it over to a topical-film firm to print and circulate, the firm to take fifty per cent. of the receipts and to bear the expense of printing and other details.

CHAPTER VIII

ABERRATIONS OF ANIMATED PHOTOGRAPHY

It has been pointed out in a previous chapter that cinematography is nothing more or less than an optical illusion. Further proof of this assertion exists in plenty. When following the projection of a picture upon the screen, one is often perplexed by a curious effect, or a movement which appears to be in opposition to all the known laws of motion. This happens not only in trick work where such odd and startling effects are introduced purposely, but in straightforward every-day topical subjects.

For instance, it must have been noticed that when a ship or railway train is in rapid movement, and is photographed from a fixed stationary point, such as the quay or platform, the moving object appears to stand out in bold relief against the background. One gathers a very comprehensive idea of its length, width, height, and the comparative size of all its integral parts, such as the guns on the ship's deck or the locomotive's cylinders. It is a curious stereoscopic effect, but at the same time is not truly so, because it is only the moving object which appears to possess solidity. The foreground and background remain as plane surfaces so that it is impossible to obtain an idea of distance. This effect arises from the fact that what might be described as the central part of the picture is moving or continually changing, thereby compelling all the objects attached to its length and breadth to assume relief in regard to the other parts of the picture.

But if the camera with which the pictures are taken is placed upon the moving object itself, then the whole of the resulting picture stands out in a truly stereoscopic manner. One gathers an impression of distance between the various objects on the screen. Everything is shown with form and solidity in precisely the same way as if one were looking through a hand stereoscope upon a photograph taken stereoscopically. This effect is due to the fact that all the planes are moving continually.

But probably the most bewildering puzzle is the moving wheel. A carriage or waggon is seen advancing across the screen from left to right, but the spokes of the wheels, on the other hand, seem to be moving in the opposite direction. At other times the spokes move in successive spasmodic jumps, or appear to be stationary, so that a curious skidding effect is produced, notwithstanding that the rim itself is seen to be revolving normally.

There have been many explanations of this extraordinary effect, and in one instance the higher mathematics were pressed into service without any great success.   The most convincing explanation known to the writer is that given him by Monsieur Lucien Bull, the assistant-director of the Marey Institute, where phenomena of this class are minutely investigated, because they accord with the work of that unique and admirable institution.   By Monsieur Bull the illusion was explained very easily, but, curiously enough, in carrying out the experiments to this end, he encountered another illusion equally strange.

To reduce the explanation to its simplest form we will suppose that a wheel has four spokes spaced equidistantly, that is, 90 degrees apart, and that the wheel is moving from right to left. As a matter of fact such an example is not the best for the purpose, but it shall be taken merely because it is the simplest to understand. An exposure is made, the wheel being photographed in the position shown in Fig. 3.   The lens is eclipsed by the shutter, and the film is jerked downwards into position in the gate so as to bring a fresh unexposed surface before the lens. While this operation is taking place, we will suppose that the wheel, continuing its forward movement, completes one quarter of a revolution.

Consequently when the second exposure is made spoke 1 has moved 90 degrees, which is the angle between each spoke. Accordingly it now occupies exactly the same position as that of spoke 2 at the time of the first exposure. Spoke 2 has moved to the position formerly occupied by

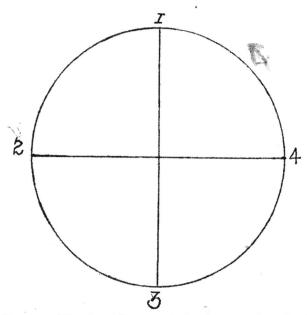

FIG. 3.—The first picture of the four-spoke wheel.

spoke 3. Spoke 3 has travelled sufficiently to to take the place of spoke 4, while 4 has gone to that of 1 (Fig. 4). If four exposures are made, and the spokes move 90 degrees each time the lens is closed, when the four pictures are thrown successively upon the screen they will look exactly alike. The spokes will appear to be quite

P.C.   H stationary, although the rim of the wheel will have moved a distance equal to its circumference across the screen. Consequently, if a dozen, a hundred, or a thousand exposures are made under these conditions, the spokes moving 90

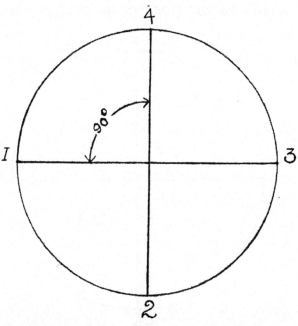

Fig. 4.—During the eclipse of the lens the spokes have moved a distance equal to the angle between them, causing the spokes apparently to stand still while the wheel is moving.

degrees between each exposure, a quaint skidding effect will be produced. All the spokes being alike the eye is unable to detect that any displacement has taken place between one exposure and another. This impression of the spokes standing still while the wheel is moving, must arise in every case in which the wheel moves sufficiently to cause the spokes to cover a distance equal to the angle between them during the interval while the lens is eclipsed by the

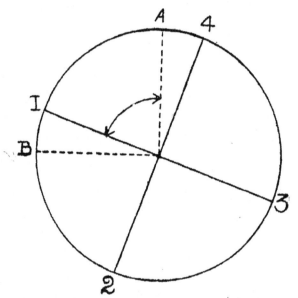

FIG. 5.—During the eclipse of the lens the spokes move less than the angle (AB) between them, producing apparent backward motion of the spokes while the wheel is running forwards.

shutter. It will happen equally whether the wheel has four, sixteen, or more spokes.

Now we will suppose that the revolving speed of the wheel is retarded, causing less than a quarter of a revolution to be completed between each exposure. The spokes, let us say, move through an angle of 85 degrees instead of 90 degrees while the lens is eclipsed. The eye at first receives the impression shown in Fig. 3. As the wheel only covers 85 degrees during the eclipse, in the second picture the eye observes that movement has occurred. Spoke 1 is now

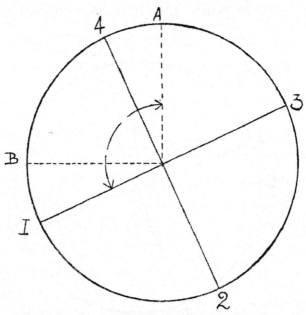

FIG. 6.—During the eclipse of the lens the spokes move more than the angle (AB) between them, and accordingly the wheel is seen to be moving naturally.

behind the point formerly occupied by spoke 2 (shown by the dotted line in Fig. 5) in the first exposure. The lens is eclipsed once more, and the spoke moves another 85 degrees. When the next picture is seen spoke 1 has fallen still farther behind the 90 degrees mark, and this indication of less movement than the right angle becomes accentuated with each succeeding exposure. Accordingly, the spokes in the successive pictures appear to be moving at a less speed than the rim of the wheel, and forthwith the eye imagines that the spokes are travelling backwards, although meantime the wheel rim is seen to be advancing across the screen. This remarkable effect is produced whenever the advance of the wheel is such as to cause the spokes to move less than the angle between them, no matter what the size of the angle may be.

We will now suppose that the revolving speed of the wheel is accelerated so as to cause more than a quarter of a revolution to be made while the lens is eclipsed—that the spokes move forward 95 degrees between each exposure. In this case, while the first picture will show the position indicated in Fig. 3, the next exposure will show spoke 1 in the position shown in Fig. 6, that is, in advance of the angle of 90 degrees and in advance of the position occupied by spoke 2—(see the dotted line)—in the first exposure. In the third picture the spoke will be shown still farther in advance of the right angle mark, and the effect will be produced of the spokes apparently gaining upon one another. When a series of pictures taken under such conditions is thrown upon the screen in rapid succession, the spokes and rim will be seen to be moving harmoniously in the forward and correct direction. Accordingly natural movement of the

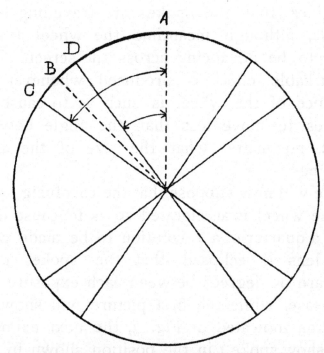

FIG. 7.—When the spokes move slightly more (AC) or slightly less (AD) than half the angle (AB) between them, during the eclipse of the lens, the curious illusion of seeing twice the number of spokes in the wheel is produced.

wheel only can be shown when the spokes of the wheel, irrespective of their number, move a distance equal to more than the angle between them.

In the course of elucidating this problem

Monsieur Bull discovered another curious optical illusion produced by the moving wheel. Still taking the four-spoke wheel as an illustration, we will suppose that between each exposure the spokes are displaced a little more or a little less than half the angle between them. As the spokes are set 90 degrees apart, the half-way point will be 45 degrees. When a succession of such pictures is thrown upon the screen, it is not four spokes which are seen, but eight (Fig. 7). Monsieur Bull is engaged upon a series of experiments to ascertain why this peculiar optical illusion should prevail, and the explanation will prove interesting.

Another interesting and more conclusive illustration of the optically illusory properties of the cinematograph was demonstrated to me by Monsieur Bull. In order to be absolutely positive that an apparatus which he uses in certain cinematographic investigations should maintain the speed he desires, he has contrived a tuning-fork control for his electric motor. This tuning-fork resembles a large trembler blade, such as is used in the high-tension accumulator and coil ignition system upon motor cars. This particular instrument is timed to make, say, 40 vibrations per second, and at this speed, of course, it emits a distinctive musical note. This tuning-fork controls the electric motor driving the apparatus. For the purpose of illustration we will suppose it to be necessary that the speed of the motor shall not exceed 40 revolutions per second. In the earliest experiments he depended upon his ear to detect whether the motor and tuning-fork were in synchrony. He varied the speed of the motor until its hum was dead in tune with that of the tuning-fork.

But, as he thought that his ear might not be infallible, he devised an ingenious synchronising apparatus based upon the cinematographic principle. A small disk of cardboard provided with two holes near its edge, at opposite points of the circumference, is mounted upon the spindle of the tiny motor. Behind this disk is placed a small adjustable mirror. A pencil of electric light is projected horizontally in such a manner that it strikes the cardboard disk at right angles, and, when a hole on the disk is brought into line with it, it passes through and falls upon the mirror. The mirror is then set so as to reflect and focus the pencil of light in a small circle upon the free vibrating extremity of the tuning-fork. Naturally a strong shadow is thrown by the latter upon the white wall behind.

In the daylight the vibration of this fork is distinctly visible, and although it is slight and rapid it can be followed without any effort. But when the room is darkened, the ray of light is thrown upon the tuning-fork from the mirror. When the motor bearing the cardboard disk is set in motion a very curious effect is produced. The pencil of light reflected against the tuning-fork becomes interrupted twice in every revolution of the disk, that is 80 times per second, so that, looking at the background upon which the tuning-fork is silhouetted, the effect produced is precisely similar to that observable upon the cinematograph screen, where the passage of the light from the lantern is interrupted by the rotary action of the shutter. If the revolving speed of the motor, that is the number of revolutions per second, is the same as the number of vibrations per second of the tuning-fork, viz. 40, the end of the fork, as one looks at the illuminated circle on the wall against which the shadow is thrown, appears to be at rest. One only needs to touch the end of the fork, however, to be certain that it is vibrating.

Now if the motor be thrown out of synchrony with the tuning-fork, even if it makes only 39 or 41 instead of 40 revolutions per second, the disturbance is shown instantly, because looking at the illuminated tuning-fork one observes it jumping spasmodically. This movement becomes more pronounced as the harmony between the revolutions of the motor and the fork is disturbed, the jumps of the blade at times being apparently of a very severe character. Moreover, curiously enough, under the illumination of the ray of light the erratic movements of the blade appear to be three or four times more severe than they really are. But as the motor revolutions and the tuning-fork vibrations are brought into synchrony, the movements grow quieter, until at last the tuning-fork once more appears to be quiescent.

The explanation of this quasi-cinematographic illusion, which is as interesting and as puzzling as that of the wheel, is very simple, for it is based indeed upon the same phenomena. As the cardboard disk is provided with two small holes spaced 180 degrees apart, the passage of the ray of light is intercepted by the opaque section of the disk 80 times per second when the motor revolutions and the tuning-fork vibrations are in absolute synchrony. The result is that at this speed the light strikes the tuning-fork each time at the instant it is at the half-way point in its oscillating travel. One hole in the disk comes before the light when the blade has completed half its movement in one direction, while the second hole comes into line with the light when the blade is at the same point on its return journey. Consequently the light falls upon the blade at the same spot every time, causing the eye to imagine that it sees the blade always in the one position as if under a steady ray of continuous light.

Hence comes its apparent quiescence. But directly the speed of the motor is altered in relation to the vibration of the tuning-fork, the rays of light catch the blade at varying points in its travel, and these changes, coming in quick succession, convey the visual idea of movement. Acceleration of the motor so that its revolving speed per second exceeds the number of the tuning-fork vibrations, causes the perceptible movements to be made more quickly, while on the other hand deceleration slows them down. In reality the eye imagines that it sees more than what actually takes place; it imagines that the blade of the fork is kicking spasmodically and viciously, whereas in fact the extent of the movement to and fro is constant and never changes.

While the experiment is peculiarly fascinating, its application is extremely useful to the worker. It offers a means of being absolutely certain about the speed at which the instrument utilised in a particular investigation is running, so that the resulting calculations may be completed without the slightest error.

CHAPTER IX

SLOWING DOWN RAPID MOVEMENTS

DURING the past few years much effort has been spent upon adapting the cinematograph so that it will record exceedingly rapid movements, such as a bullet in flight. Some popular films of this character have been placed on the market, and, in order to attract the public, have been colloquially described as "quicker-than-thought" or "quicker-than-the-eye" movements. Strictly speaking both the latter designations are erroneous, especially in regard to the eye, inasmuch as if a bullet fired from a rifle were brilliant white the eye would be able to follow its flight with ease, notwithstanding the fact that it may issue from the muzzle with a travelling speed of 2,000 feet or more per second.

So far as the moving-picture camera is concerned it is obvious that the ordinary machine could not be operated with sufficient speed to film a bullet in flight, or even to catch the flap of the wings of a small insect, such as a house-fly or bee. It would be impossible to jerk the film through the gate with sufficient speed to take perhaps five thousand pictures per second—the mechanism, and more particularly the film, would break down before a fiftieth of the number of pictures were taken in the space of one second.

Accordingly, great ingenuity has been displayed by cinematograph investigators in the evolution of a means of snapping such extremely rapid movements at sufficient speed to make the films interesting or scientifically useful. This particular branch of the craft was developed first by Monsieur Lucien Bull, of the Marey Institute, who designed a novel and ingenious camera capable of taking up to two thousand pictures per second.[1] With this apparatus many wonderful films have been obtained, and such a fascinating field of study has been revealed that attempts are being made in all directions to secure "quicker-than-thought" films that would have been thought ten years ago to be photographically impossible. Monsieur Bull is developing his idea in order to be in a position to obtain longer records of a subject, and also to take the photographs at a higher rate of speed. Professor Cranz, a German experimenter, also has carried out some novel experiments on the same lines, and has designed a system whereby

[1] See " Moving Pictures : How they are Made and Worked," Chapter XXIV., page 264.

he is able to take a photograph in the ten-millionth part of a second.

This particular phase of cinematographic investigation is wonderfully fascinating, and from the private worker's point of view it is additionally attractive because it offers him an opportunity to display his ingenuity. It is only by individual effort and the mutual communication of ideas that perfection can be achieved, and in this one field there is great scope. There are many problems which have to be solved, many of which are peculiar to this particular study. It involves a combination of the electrical and cinematographic expert, since dependence has to be placed upon the electric spark for illumination, and also upon electricity for operating the mechanism.

In such work as this the time factor is a most important feature. Obviously, from the scientific point of view, it is essential to have some reliable means of determining the fraction of a second in which each picture is taken and also the period which elapses between the successive pictures. In the system devised by Monsieur Lucien Bull a tuning-fork is used. The vibrations of this fork per second are known, and as the two ends of the fork are reproduced in each image, it is by no means difficult to calculate the time factor.

Dr. E. J. Marey insisted strongly on the importance of this registration of time. It is obviously essential in many kinds of scientific work. Marey during his life investigated some very rapid natural movements such as those of a pigeon's wings during flight. Such a film would have been useless from the scientific point of view, unless there were some means of showing in what interval of time each successive picture was taken, and also the period which elapsed between each exposure. Knowledge of these two facts enables one to tell the time occupied in making a complete flap of the wing, and the physical changes which take place in the shape of the wing to accommodate the bird to different conditions, and it also enables the investigator to trace the motion photographically lost while the lens is eclipsed to permit the film to be moved forward.

To this end Marey devised an interesting type of clock. It consisted of a dial provided with one large revolving hand which was driven by ordinary clockwork. The face of the dial was marked off into twenty equal divisions, each of which corresponded to one-twentieth part of a second. This "chronoscope" as it was called, was placed near the object under cinematographic study, so that both the movement of the clock-hand and that of the object were photographed simultaneously. This system of timing motions it may be pointed out has been revived ın a similar form by Mr. Frank Gilbreth in connection with "micro-motion" study described in another chapter.

Marey also evolved a means of adapting the camera so as to enable him to take the pictures at a speed exceeding sixteen per second. He did not change the mechanism of the camera very radically, but was able to secure as many as one hundred and ten pictures per second His arrangement of the camera was very simple, as shown on the plate opposite. The film travelled intermittently, its arrest for each exposure being very abrupt. In the camera were two cylinders C and C¹ between which the film passed, and these cylinders revolved in opposite directions and towards one another. As the two peripheries of the cylinders were brought together the film was gripped and was moved forward by friction, somewhat in the manner of the clutch-action which was adopted in the very first moving-picture cameras. But each cylinder was provided with eight flattened sections, of equal length, disposed equidistantly. Consequently, when two opposing flat surfaces came together the grip on the film was momentarily released, and the film stopped, though the cylinders continued their rotary motion. By the

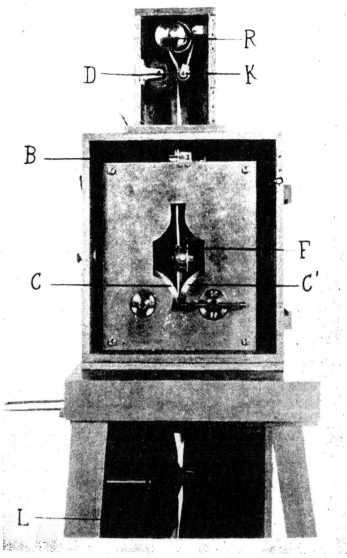

R

D K

B

F

C C'

L

MAREY'S APPARATUS FOR TAKING MOVING-PICTURES OF
RAPID MOVEMENTS.

(For explanation see p. 112.)

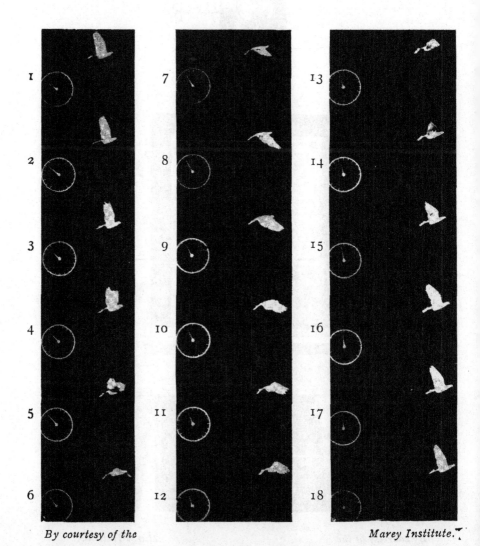

By courtesy of the   *Marey Institute.*

CINEMATOGRAPHING RAPID MOVEMENTS.

The complete beat of a pigeon's wing secured by Dr. Marey in eighteen pictures, and taken, according to the "chronoscope" in the corner, in $\frac{3}{20}$ths of a second.

incorporation of gear trains the number of revolutions could be varied up to about seventeen or eighteen per second. In the camera, above the lens was a small device whereby the sudden and complete stoppage of the film was assured during the periods when it was not gripped by the cylinders below. Another similar device was introduced at F above the window, through which the mechanism at the gate was visible, and this also pressed lightly upon the film to counteract all the vibrations set up from its quick intermittent movement. The unexposed film was mounted upon a spool in the removable box R in the usual manner, but before being fed into the camera it passed between two other friction disks D and K, and was then fed through the camera mechanism and out at the bottom into a second removable spool box L, where it was wound in after exposure. This lower box also contained two friction disks similar to those in the unexposed film box, and the larger of these cylinders in the lower box, like D in the upper or unexposed box, was driven by the revolving handle, through belts and pulleys.

It was a very simple apparatus. Although it was open to the objection that the film might slip while photographs were being taken at high speed, Marey proved strikingly successful in his use of it, his pictures being wonderfully steady, even when taken at a speed of one hundred and forty per second. In photographing the beat of a pigeon's wings he secured a complete cycle of motion in eighteen pictures, which, by reference to the chronoscope visible in the same field, shows that they were recorded in three-twentieths of a second.

Such an adaptation of the camera could be used successfully to-day for what might be described, somewhat paradoxically, as slow rapid movements. But it would be better to secure a more positive and simple means of moving the film forward. Of course the main advantage of the friction disk system is that the film suffers no damage as it moves. In an ordinary camera, working on the conventional claw principle, there would be a tendency to tear the perforations when the pictures exceeded sixty or so per second, and it would prove difficult in some instances to ensure the absolute quiescence and steadiness of the film during exposure. With the Geneva stop system of moving the film, a steady smooth movement is more easily obtained than with the claw mounted upon a sharp eccentric.

For such work where there is no desire to exceed two hundred pictures or so per second, the ideal camera is that which has been perfected by Monsieur M. P. Noguès, of the Marey Institute.

In general appearance this camera resembles the ordinary machine. It was designed specially for the purpose of field work, for which Monsieur Bull's camera is not suitable. In Monsieur Bull's camera the illumination is effected by means of

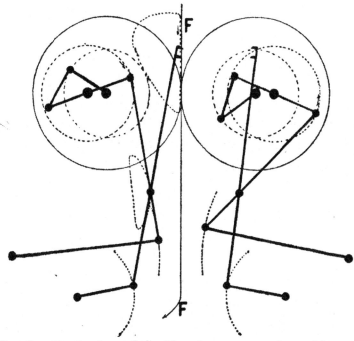

FIG. 8.—Mechanism of the Noguès camera, wherewith up to two hundred and forty pictures per second can be taken.

the electric spark, and it is impossible by this means to light a large field.

In Monsieur Noguès' camera there are two claws, each mounted upon its own eccentric, and the film passes between them. The claws do not work together. That is to say, they do not engage the film simultaneously on both sides, but work alternately. When one is engaged with the film the other is in the out position. Without entering into a technical description of the mechanism it may be stated that there is an articulated lever system, so designed as to give the claws an irregular D-shaped trajectory, which is very rapid and abrupt, the ascent of the claw to re-engage with the film being sharper and quicker than is possible in the orthodox design. The general design of the claw mechanism and its method of operation may be gathered from a reference to Fig. 8, wherein the paths described by the moving parts are indicated clearly. The handle whereby the camera is operated is turned at the normal speed of two revolutions per second, but this, owing to the gearing, causes ninety or more downward jerks to be imparted to the film F during each second. This makes one hundred and eighty film movements by the two claws per second, and consequently one hundred and eighty exposures.

Notwithstanding the high speed at which the celluloid ribbon is moved through the camera, there are no signs whatever of tearing. Furthermore, the film, during the brief period of exposure —from $\frac{1}{360}$th to $\frac{1}{480}$th part of a second—remains perfectly steady and quiet in the gate.

The first camera built on this principle had

a maximum speed of one hundred and eighty pictures per second, but by modifying certain details it was found possible to increase the velocity in a subsequent machine to two hundred and two hundred and forty pictures per second. This represents a far higher speed than has ever yet been attained with the ordinary moving-picture apparatus. The machine is no larger than the ordinary type, although, owing to the rapidity with which the pictures are taken, the externally fitting film-box system is adopted, so as to provide a supply of about 700 feet of film for exposure.

In projection on the screen the speed is reduced to about one-twentieth or more of the rate of the exposure. The results are far superior to any which have yet been seen upon the screen. The movements are steadier and more con-tinuous, inasmuch as the proportion of lost movement is about one-twentieth of what it is with the orthodox instrument. The result is that one sees upon the screen many phases of movement which otherwise escape detection or are only partially shown under present cinemato-graphing conditions. Owing to the gearing and the balance of the moving parts the operation of this camera is not more fatiguing than that of the ordinary instrument ; indeed, it runs far more easily and lightly. The camera has been evolved for the express purpose of reinvestigating many of the studies conducted by Marey, which, owing to the imperfect appliances at his disposal, are possibly incomplete.

But it may be asked, where is the demand for pictures taken at such a speed? In reply it is only necessary to point out that such photographing speeds are indispensable in studying the motions of the smaller members of the animal kingdom. For instance, an amateur recently prepared a film showing the life and habits of lizards. They were taken at the normal speed of sixteen pictures per second, which the operator judged to be sufficient. But when the pictures were shown upon the screen, the very motions which are the most interesting, such as the movement of the tongue, jerk of the head, and so forth, were lost. Similarly, another film depicted the chameleon, but failed to catch the instantaneous throw of its tongue. On the other hand, when the pictures were taken at the accelerated speed of fifty to eighty per second, the results were strikingly different. Not only were they more complete, but they were smoother, more continuous, and more natural; in fact, they were practically identical with those which the human eye observes in the creatures themselves.

Phases of natural movement, capable of being recorded at speeds ranging between eighty and two hundred per second, are the most promising spheres of moving-picture activity at the present moment. Nature study never fails to arouse enthusiasm, while from the operator's point of view it is indescribably fascinating. Something unexpected is secured at every turn of the handle. The portrayal of Nature stirs the emotions of wonder, it is true to fact, and it often introduces the spectator to something about which he has read but which he never has seen. Consequently, so far as life is concerned, the pictures should never be taken at less than forty to fifty per second, unless one is contented to have a mere distorted impression of what actually takes place. Even moving-pictures of the snail or tortoise, generally considered to move very slowly, should never be photographed at a less speed, because these have actions which cannot be caught at sixteen pictures per second.

Generally speaking, the smaller the live subject under investigation, the more rapid should be the photographing speed. The movements of a bee's wings cannot be caught at sixteen or even two hundred pictures per second. This was proved some time ago when Monsieur Lucien Bull, by the aid of his electric spark system, and special camera, obtained a series of photos showing how a bee regains its normal balance when it is upset. For this purpose a bee was launched from the special apparatus used in connection with the camera, with its equilibrum very seriously disturbed. So rapid was its recovery that twenty pictures taken in succession at the above speed served to illustrate the whole operation, the final photograph showing the bee in normal flight. This was the first occasion wherein this peculiar phenomenon had been photographically recorded, and the unique character of the achievement may be realised from the fact that the bee regained its balance in the infinitesimal period of approximately the hundredth part of a second.

Even in photographing a man, to show rapid walking motion, a speed of sixteen pictures per second is far from adequate. If he happens to be walking at four miles an hour quite 75 per cent. of the motion is lost, and the movement portrayed under these conditions is spasmodic and jerky. For a natural cinematographic record of a man walking, at the present orthodox rate of sixteen pictures per second, his pace should not exceed a mile an hour. Therefore to film a man walking at four miles an hour the photographing speed should not be less than sixty-four pictures per second.

Though the ultra-rapid movement involves the use of intricate electrical apparatus, it is a peculiarly absorbing study. The appliances required are necessarily expensive, but, since it is virtually an untouched province, enormous opportunities await the patient worker. It is additionally attractive because each worker is to a very great extent dependent upon his own ingenuity in the design of efficient auxiliaries and secondary apparatus. It is this wide scope for individual initiative which causes rapid cinematography to be so keenly appreciated by investigators, and, as results have shown, their discoveries when popularised make a very deep impression on the public.

Of course, in projection, it is useless to attempt to throw the successive pictures upon the screen at anything approaching the speed at which they were snapped. If the flight of a bullet recorded at say ten thousand images per second, were projected at a corresponding speed, nothing would be seen. So, in projection, the speed is slowed down ; the subject photographed at two thousand pictures per second is thrown upon the screen and brought to the cyc at the rate of sixteen pictures per second. The bullet moves across the screen with the pace of a snail. The wings of a dragon fly, which in life make several hundred oscillations per second, appear to move as sluggishly as those of a barn-door fowl. But the detail and the complex movements are recorded ; the eye sees and follows something which has formerly been beyond its powers.

If it is desired to reduce the speed to its absolute slowest point, so as to facilitate even closer study, the operator can take advantage, to an extreme degree, of the phenomenon of the persistence of vision. This has been done by Monsieur Lucien Bull. It is impossible to reduce the speed of projection to less than sixteen pictures per second, for this is the lowest rate at which the laws of persistence will allow of an appearance of continuous motion. Yet there is an ingenious way of obtaining the equivalent of a speed of eight pictures per second, and this without either disturbing the apparently lifelike movement or producing any flicker. The method is by duplicating each separate picture of the negative upon the positive. That is to say each negative picture is printed twice in succession upon the positive, so that 12 inches of film, which normally would carry sixteen successive and different pictures carries in this case only eight. When projected upon the screen, at the rate of sixteen pictures per second, the eye fails to detect that it is seeing every picture twice. This might almost be described as an optical illusion, and it makes another interesting proof that the eye can be deluded by cinematography. Monsieur Bull, after having found that the eye did not observe that two identical pictures were shown in succession, endeavoured to carry multiplication still farther. He found, however, that a pair of pictures was the limit. When three identical pictures were shown in succession the impression upon the eye was too long. The movement from triplet to triplet gave a disjointed effect such as arises in ordinary projection when the speed is too slow.

CHAPTER X

THE preceding chapter described how it is possible to photograph extraordinarily rapid movements and to slow down in projection so as to enable the eye to follow them. Now I will go to the other extreme and show how the very slowest movements can be accelerated and thrown upon the screen in continuous motion. This feature has proved one of the most popular in the whole range of cinematography, for it has enabled the public to follow, within the course of a few minutes, such wonderful and apparently impossible studies as the growth of a plant from the germination of the seed and the appearance of the leaves to the bursting of the bloom and the formation of the seed for the propagation of the species.

The speeding-up of relatively slow movements has become a favourite branch of research among cinematograph workers mainly because it is simple, inexpensive, and comparatively easy. The worker needs to develop only one special faculty. That is patience, for the recording of a single subject may easily extend over a period of a month or so, and the camera has to be kept going night and day to produce a faithful record. It is a field which the amateur can follow very profitably. It puts no great tax on his skill. The risk of failure is slight, and the films thus obtained, if worked out upon popular or instructive lines, are certain to command a ready market.

For this work one may use the ordinary £5 ($25) camera. It illustrates the fact that cinematography is nothing more nor less than a string of successive snap-shots, for the principle is that which is generally described as " one turn one picture." That is to say, instead of the handle being turned continuously as in taking a topical subject, it is moved at stated intervals, and only sufficiently to make one exposure and to jerk the film downwards the required distance ready to receive the succeeding image. It virtually resolves cinematography into ordinary snap-shot or Kodak photography.

This development, like many others widely practised in the moving-picture world to-day, has issued from the Marey Institute. It was there exploited in the usual manner for the study of natural movement and phenomena. In the early days of the present century, even before the picture palace came into vogue, the workers of this institution produced a short length of film

showing the opening of the blossom of a convolvulus. Although this film is some ten years old
it would be difficult even now to improve upon
it. The opening movement of the petals is so
steady and perfect as to suggest that the exposure
was not intermittent but continuous.

In these particular studies success in the main
depends upon the apparatus employed for the
periodical exposure of the film and the judgment
shown in deciding the lapse of time between the
successive exposures. Naturally this varies
according to the characteristics of the subject
under investigation. A mushroom, for instance,
demands exposure at briefer intervals than would
be necessary for filming the growth of a grain of
wheat. The timing is perhaps the most difficult
part of the undertaking, because if it is not
gauged to a nicety the movement on the screen
is apt to be unnatural, the growth taking place
in a series of sudden jerks instead of proceeding
slowly, steadily and gracefully. Many a first-
class film of this character has been ruined
because the interval between the exposures has
been too long to bring about the necessary
blending together of the motions in the successive
pictures. No hard and fast rule can be laid down
to guide the worker. Experience and close study
of the subject being photographed can alone
enable this factor to be determined.

The auxiliary apparatus to ensure the exposures being made at regular intervals need not be of an intricate character. The simpler the means, the more likely is the result to be successful. Clockwork mechanism can be devised to open the shutter at stated intervals, but this system suffers from one serious disadvantage. The mechanism must be wound up regularly, and when a long study is in progress, extending over a fortnight or a month, the worker is apt to overlook this indispensable duty. There is one worker who generally uses a water motor, and has found it very reliable; but it cannot be safely left, and it ceases to act if the public water supply be cut off.

The most reliable agent for such work is electricity. When the Marey Institute first embarked upon these tedious subjects a very elaborate apparatus was employed. It was like a gallows, being in reality a massive wooden frame (see illustration facing page 128) fitted with a pulley. A rope passed over this pulley, and to one end was attached a weight P. The other end passed round a small winch T, to which the camera C was connected. Upon the spindle connecting these two parts of the mechanism was a small wing-piece L, one of the extremities of which rested upon a vertical spindle E connected with an electro-magnet F. In the electro-magnet circuit was a small water-balancer B having two cells and a see-saw motion. This was driven by a stream of water flowing from the tap of the tank R. The flow of water from the tap could be regulated.

When the elevated cell of the balancer was filled, its weight caused it to fall. As it fell the electric circuit of the battery V was closed. This caused the small vertical rod E to be drawn downwards by the electro-magnet F. The descent of the rod allowed the leaf L to fall. The make and break in the electro-magnet was instantaneous, so that the vertical rod E immediately returned to its normal position, with the result that, when the wing came round, after completing a revolution, it was stopped, and remained there until the second cell of the water-balancer, filling and falling in its turn, repeated the cycle of operations. As the rod carrying the wing L was the common axis of the winch and the driving mechanism of the camera the release of the wing brought the strain of the weight P upon the cord, and thereby moved the camera driving mechanism a complete revolution. Thus it conformed to the " one-turn-one-picture " movement. It was a combination of weight-driven and electrical mechanism, and, though apparently complicated and certainly cumbersome, it was satisfactory because it completed its work with

THE ELABORATE APPARATUS CONTRIVED AT THE MAREY
INSTITUTE TO TAKE THE FIRST MOVING-PICTURES OF
THE OPENING OF A FLOWER.

(For explanation see p. 127.)

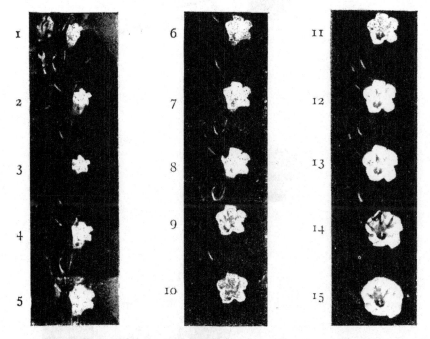

THE FIRST MOTION-PICTURES OF AN OPENING FLOWER.

Taken at the Marey Institute. The complete opening of a convolvulus is shown in fifteen pictures.

unerring steadiness and regularity. As the weight P descended a very small distance for each exposure a single winding-up was sufficient to drive the mechanism for several hours. The intervals between the exposures could be varied by turning the tap on or off, thereby changing the volume of water flowing into the balancer. The thinner the water stream the longer the period required to fill the cell, the longer the interval between each see-saw, and obviously the greater the lapse of time between each exposure. Similarly the time intervals between each exposure could be shortened by turning on the tap so that the cell became filled more quickly.

In the Marey Institute investigations with the convolvulus, which was placed on a chair a short distance from the lens of the camera, sixteen successive snap-shots were made in the hour. These pictures, taken at intervals of four minutes, show the complete opening of the flower, the phases in the successive pictures blending so well together as to convey the impression that the pictures were taken at the normal speed.

A striking contrast to the bulky, weighty, and massive apparatus employed ten years ago to photograph intermittently the opening of a flower is the latest device which is employed at this Institute for this work. It is a small, light compact contrivance driven by a kind of carriage clock. This clock actuates two levers whereby electric contacts are made at predeter mined intervals to open and close the lens. This mechanism can be set so as to give exposures at intervals ranging from a minute to several hours, and will run for twenty-four hours without attention. The apparatus is as accurate as it is ingenious.

It is obvious, however, in such work, that a great deal depends upon the personality of the worker himself. If he is skilful he will find no difficulty in devising a reliable timing apparatus which he can trust for hours together. But the simpler the character of the appliances the more trustworthy will they prove, because the reduction in the number of the component parts will decrease their liability to derangement and irregular action.

Seeing that exposures have to be continued at the predetermined intervals throughout the whole twenty-four hours, arrangements must be made for artificial illumination during the night. This should not prove a difficult problem. There is a wide range of illuminants—electricity, gas, acetylene, etc.—from which a choice can be made according to the circumstances of the case. Thus a worker living in country districts may find a difficulty in obtaining electric current or coal gas, in which case he must rely upon acetylene, or a petrol gas flame, in conjunction with an incandescent mantle, or even an electric battery and flash-lamp with a reflector.

If electricity or coal gas are available from public supply sources there need be no anxieties whatever. A metallic filament incandescent electric lamp of high power is quite sufficient for the purpose, and if there is need for a con-centrated strong light it can be obtained by mounting the lamp within a parobolic reflector, such as is used for automobiles. Coal gas with an incandescent burner and mantle is just as efficient, and concentration in this case can be managed in the same way with a reflector. But it is necessary to make sure that no draughts play upon the gas flame, as the intensity of the light might thus be greatly impoverished.

Acetylene is a very useful and powerful illuminant when all else fails. It is the nearest artificial approach to sunlight. Petrol gas with an incandescent mantle will be found just as good as ordinary coal gas, while there are many cheap lamps well adapted for its use. If all these alternatives are lacking there is the electric flash lamp working with the dry battery. A tiny metallic filament incandescent bulb mounted within a parabolic reflector will give a light of intense brilliancy. But the exhaustion of the battery causes the value of this light to diminish

K 2

in a relatively short time, so it is well not to let it burn continuously. There should be a means of producing the flash only at the moment the timing apparatus makes the exposure. In one application of this system the flash and the movement of the shutter are controlled by an electro-magnet, arranged in such a manner that the lamp lights up a fraction of a second before the shutter is moved. Thus the object under study is in the full glare of the light before the film is exposed. Of course, if a high capacity accumulator can be obtained, such as that of the latest Edison Nickel type, the light may be left burning continuously. But when there is already an electrical system of actuating the shutter it is a simple matter to incorporate a means of limiting the contact in the lamp to the moment of the exposure.

For the average worker, however, the electrical system is too costly. He will usually prefer a form of light which can be allowed to burn continuously through the night. Even the longest night will not consume a very great quantity of current or gas. Also, unless some very accurate mechanism is used for controlling the intermittent operation of the light, there is always a chance that the exposure and the illumination may fail to synchronise, and thus an excellent film might be ruined.

The "one-turn-one-picture" movement has to be adopted for many subjects other than flowers. For instance, it is necessary in filming the movements of the star-fish, in evolution phenomena such as the emergence of a chicken from its shell, and in the case of certain minute organisms which can be cinematographed only with the aid of a microscope. But the same broad principles apply in each case; there is equal need for time and patience, while complete success can only be achieved by careful observation and ingenuity. There are critical moments in such work and the unexpected frequently happens. Unless the operator is equal to the emergency weeks of tedious labour may be wasted.

The study of exceedingly slow movements offers a very promising field to the patient worker. A film which occupies a month to photograph, and entails an exposure once every thirty minutes, produces a film only 90 feet in length. In projection it passes across the screen in a minute and a half. This means that a process of Nature is condensed into one thirty-seven-thousandth part of the time it actually took, and its presentation on the screen is a remarkable triumph. But at first sight the minute and a half seems a very slight return for the time and labour expended. This is one of the principal reasons why the professional cinematographer displays a marked aversion to the recording of slow movements. On the other hand, it offers unique attractions to the private investigator, for the time occupied in preparing a film that reveals the wonders of Nature invariably commands a high price if it has the elements of popularity or novelty.

CHAPTER XI

It has already been pointed out that the intermittent method of taking cinematograph pictures results in the loss of certain motions which occur during the interval when the lens is eclipsed by the shutter. A similar loss is experienced by the eye, in daily life, when it blinks. In the case of blinking, of course, the proportion of movement which escapes observation is exceedingly small. But in cinematography practically one half of the movement is lost. When very rapid movements are being investigated these losses become appreciable—in fact the most vital part of a motion may be missed during the $\frac{1}{32}$ part of a second during which the lens is covered by the shutter.

There are many fields in which cinematography as at present practised is quite useless owing to this intermittent eclipse of the lens. Suppose that the behaviour of a rapidly moving piston rod is under observation. With the ordinary type of moving picture camera and process the results are quite misleading. The piston travels so rapidly, perhaps at a rate of 8,000 lineal feet per minute, that with sixteen pictures per second only a very small proportion of the work would be recorded.

This deficiency, however, is remedied by another development in chronophotography. This is the continuous cinematographic record, the outstanding feature of which is the elimination of the revolving shutter and the intermittent movement of the film, in favour of a lens that is constantly open, a sensitized ribbon that moves steadily and continuously all the time the experiment is in progress.

Marey, in the course of his momentous investigations with animated photography, used this system for a number of experiments in which an intermittent exposure would not have afforded sufficiently precise results. Recent experiments have substantiated Marey's contentions upon this point, and have shown how unreliable are the results obtained with sixteen pictures per second where extraordinary precision is required. An effort was made to remove the drawback of the intermittent method by writing in, or divining, the movement which occurred during the periods of eclipse, but this method, in turn, was found to be unreliable. There are some motions which it is impossible to imagine or anticipate, even if they do occur in the

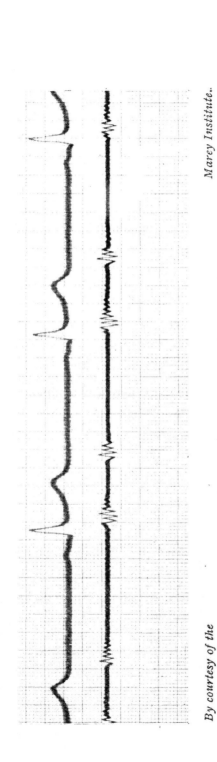

By courtesy of the

Marey Institute.

CONTINUOUS MOVING-PICTURE RECORDS OF THE BEATS AND SOUNDS OF THE HEART.

Electro-cardiogramme of a normal person. The upper line refers to the heart beats; the lower line is a photographic record of the heart sounds. These wonderful pictures are rendered possible by Dr. Einthoven's string galvanometer in conjunction with Mr. Lucien Bull's ingenious camera.

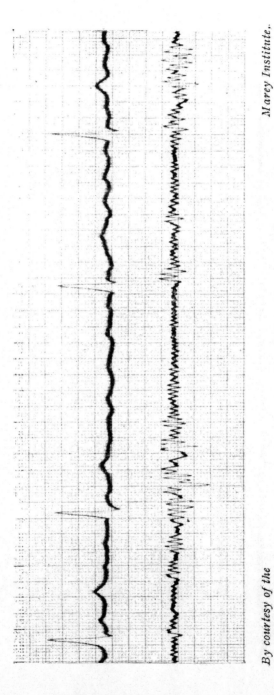

CONTINUOUS MOVING-PICTURES OF THE HEART BEATS OF AN EXCITED PERSON.

The upper line shows the palpitations occurring at irregular intervals, while the lower line is a cinematographic record of the heart sounds.

one-thirty-second or one-sixty-fourth part of a second.

Under these circumstances the continuous photographing system is now very extensively employed. It has undergone many wonderful developments and achieved extraordinary success.

One of the most interesting and marvellous of its triumphs was won with the extremely sensitive "string" galvanometer, which was invented by the eminent Dutch scientist, Professor Einthoven. This particular apparatus has been of incalculable value to the medical profession, and Monsieur Lucien Bull has constructed a special camera with the idea of obtaining permanent and continuous cinematographic records of the experiments conducted by means of it.

The apparatus employed for this particular sphere of operations is of a somewhat involved character. Fundamentally the camera is that which was designed by Monsieur Bull for photographing the flight of insects at the rate of two thousand pictures per second, but it has been modified to suit the new conditions. The reason why it offers the best chance of securing a continuous record is that its sensitized ribbon is mounted upon a drum, a single winding of which produces a photographic record about 3 feet 6 inches in length.

The principle of the Einthoven string galvanometer may be described roughly in a few words. There is a very fine conducting wire, or fibre, of platinum or silvered quartz, which is stretched across the magnetic field of the galvanometer. It is extremely thin, being virtually a hair. Now, when an electric current, ever so slight, is transmitted through this fibre, or string, as it is called by the inventor, it is deflected from its position of rest, the extent of the deviation varying with the strength of the electrical disturbance. When a slight current is sent through the string it may betray the fact with no more than a slight tremor, but a stronger current will cause it to move violently.

A pencil of light, from an electric arc lamp, is transmitted through the galvanometer in such a way that the string is brilliantly lighted. An enlarged image of the string is then thrown upon the sensitized ribbon in the camera by means of a powerful microscope lens.

Seeing that the time and distance measurements in such delicate experiments as these are of the first importance, the sensitized surface upon which the record is printed—paper or film—is calibrated photographically while the experiment is proceeding. It is divided into small squares, the longitudinal lines referring to the time factor, while the transverse lines indicate the extent of the movement of the quartz thread.

This continuous record system is of inestimable value in connection with physiological researches when details concerning the beating of the heart are desired. A person who places a finger of each hand upon the extremities of the string, witnesses the recording of his own heart beats. For the brief period between each beat the string remains quiescent in its normal position, and the record of the same, the enlarged shadow thrown by the pencil of light through the microscope lens, is made upon the sensitized surface within the camera in the form of a steady straight line. The beat of the heart sends an impulse of electricity through the galvanometer, and causes the string to deviate rapidly. As the pencil of light is shining continuously through the microscope lens of the instrument, it stands to reason that the slightest tremor of the thread, accentuated in the shadow, must be recorded. No vibration is too slight to be caught. Not only is the extent of the vibration photographed and capable of being calculated by means of the calibration, but, as the sensitized ribbon is travelling continuously past the lens, the duration of the vibration is photographed as well.

In the case of a normal and healthy person the number of vibrations on the record, corresponding to heart-beats, will average about 80 per minute, and their extent or amplitude will remain comparatively even. But if the person is in bad health, excited, or exhausted, the palpitations will be depicted in the most erratic manner, both as regards their occurrence and their force. One very powerful palpitation, for instance, may be followed by a comparatively long interval of quiescence, succeeded by several spasmodic short movements at brief unequal periods.

From the medical point of view the perfection of the system offers illimitable opportunities. In the hospital, where a patient may be lying in a critical condition, the surgeon can have a continuous record of the state of his pulse without its being felt by hand at intervals. The physician, in unusual or baffling cases of disease, can have a photographic record of the pulse and heart movements from the moment the symptoms develop until the patient either dies or recovers. It also enables the physician to be informed as to how the invalid is responding to his treatment. Hitherto, the practice has been to feel the pulse at varying specified intervals, to commit the readings to a chart, and then to connect the points by lines so as to show at a glance whether heart movement has accelerated or decelerated, and to what degree. Such charts are satisfactory so far as they go, but they may be erroneous, because the action of the heart may have fluctuated between the readings. With the

continuous photographic system, however, guess-
work does not enter into the issue at all. The
complete story is set down in an unimpeachable
graphic manner.

Perhaps the most extraordinary feature of this
development is that the very sounds of the heart
palpitations can be committed to a sensitized
surface in a continuous manner. The principle is
much the same as in the case of the record of the
heart's movements. There is a small light disk
provided with an aperture, mounted upon a
stand. Across this aperture is stretched a thread
of platinum or quartz. This instrument is placed
in the horizontal path of a pencil of light, between
the camera and the source of illumination, so that
the ray passes through the aperture of the disk
to enter the lens of the camera. Consequently
the shadow of the quartz thread is thrown upon
the sensitized surface in the camera.

A film of soapy water is spread over the
aperture in the disk, and this, of course, comes
into contact with the quartz thread. The
provision of this film in reality converts the disk
into a very sensitive diaphragm. Now a stethoscope is placed over the patient's heart, the
opposite end of which is connected to the disk in
such a way as to bear upon the surface of the
soap bubble. When the heart beats the noise
which is set up thereby is received by the

stethoscope and conveyed to the soap bubble.
The bubble, being very sensitive, responds to
the sound movement in greater or less degree.
As it vibrates, it naturally moves the quartz
thread with it, and the moving shadow of the
string is caught by the photographic film in the
camera.

In this manner the surgeon or observer can
have a permanent continuous record of the sound
of the heart beats converted into movement, and
from the regularity of the oscillations he is able
to tell whether the heart is beating regularly. If
desired, the record of both the heart-beat as
demonstrated by the galvanometer, and the
sound of the palpitation as indicated by the soap
bubble diaphragm, may be obtained upon one
chart, and, in synchrony, so as to set a double
check upon the observations.

The chronophotography of continuous movement has been brought to a high stage of
perfection by the searching experiments of
Professor Einthoven. From the physiological
point of view he has contributed most valuable
data concerning the heart, for his experiments
have been with subjects of all ages and in
varying conditions of health. The investigations
have been extended to animals also, showing the
differences in heart beating phenomena between
the various members of the animal kingdom.

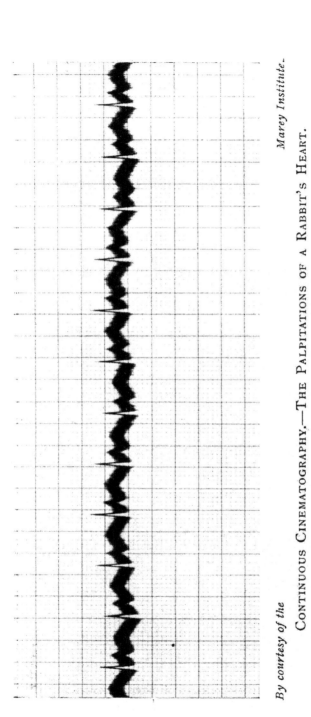

By courtesy of the   *Marey Institute.*

CONTINUOUS CINEMATOGRAPHY.—THE PALPITATIONS OF A RABBIT'S HEART.

The vertical lines indicate the extent of the heart beat, while the horizontal lines give the time interval.

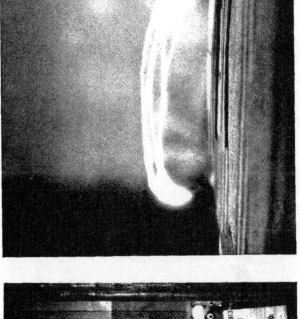

LINES OF LIGHT INDICATING TO-AND-FRO HAND MOVEMENTS.

THE STEREO-MOTION ORBIT OF A MACHINIST'S HAND.

The latest development in Micro-motion Study. A small electric incandescent lamp is attached to the workman's hand, and the lines of light photographed.

There is an increasing tendency to adopt continuous cinematography in preference to the intermittent motion for many other phases of particular study, especially where very fine results are desired.   One mechanical engineer has applied the method to the measurement of the deflection of bridges when undergoing tests. Monsieur Deslandres adopted a combination of stylography and chronophotography for recording the vibrations in metal bridges under varying conditions of traffic as far back as 1892, but the direct cinematograph record is to be preferred. Sometimes a camera has been used in combination with the existing processes of observations, so that a photograph of the actual movement and of its extent is obtained simultaneously, while the calibration of the sensitized surface, or the introduction of a clock, like that used by Marey, enables the time intervals to be accurately determined.

Another ingenious form of continuous record, which was made many years ago by Soret and Georges Demeny, the collaborator of Marey, has been revived in an improved form by Mr. Frank B. Gilbreth, the eminent American authority on motion study.   In this case a moving film is not absolutely essential, but under certain conditions it is to be preferred.   The object of the study is the tracing of motions with a view to their improvement and expedition, or the elimination of unnecessary actions, so that the particular task may be achieved in less time and with reduced exertion.

A stationary plate may be used, and the path of the motion is indicated by a ribbon of light from a small electric incandescent lamp which is attached to the hand or other limb of the subject. In this instance the plate presents an apparent jumble of lines, but by the aid of a magnifying glass the complete cycle of movements can be followed from end to end. When the photographs are taken upon a stationary plate, however, it is necessary that they should be taken stereoscopically, so that relief may be given to the picture to enable the movement to be followed correctly. The hand or limb may not be visible in the photograph, but that is a minor detail, because the path it has described is indicated by the lines of light. When the subject is continually advancing, where it does not double back upon itself, a slowly moving film will supply a complete and perfect graphic record of its progress. But in all such experiments the timing element must be incorporated, or the record will have little practical value, and will provide no conclusive evidence.

A novel application of this method was carried out by Demeny several years ago. The scope of

the investigation was the study of the characteristic walks and gaits incidental to certain
maladies.   Patients suffering from rheumatism
and other complaints which interfere with the
natural walking motions were taken into a
darkened room.   Incandescent electric lights
were attached to their shoulders, heads, and
other parts of their bodies, and these were
photographed as the subjects moved about the
darkened room.   The results upon the sensitized
surface were merely the paths described by the
moving lights.   There have been many applications of the continuous record, especially to the
work of testing physical, chemical, or electrical
phenomena.   The observer is certain to obtain a
correct result.   This has been shown in certain
microscopical observations where the movements
are extremely rapid, and where a graphic outline
is more important than the photographic detail
of the subject.

The great advantage of the continuous cinematographic system is that it records every
movement.   Even the slightest vibrations will be
indicated, and upon a large or small scale according to the rapidity with which the travelling
sensitized surface is moved through the camera.
Comparative investigation between this and the
other systems has proved that the continuous
cinematograph shows many motions which the

former systems lose. It has introduced the investigator to many curious phenomena of which he was previously ignorant.

One thing must be emphasised. It is the salient difference between the ordinary cinematographic method and the continuously moving film process. The first records upon the film a complete picture of the subject. The second records only the path or trajectory of a *single point*, or at the utmost of a number of points, of the subject under observation. This remark does not refer to the method of cinematographing with the electric spark, which is a totally different and special application of the art.

CHAPTER XII

WITH the perfection of radio-photography it was not surprising that the cinematograph investigator pressed this new development into service. It opened up a wide and fascinating field for moving pictures. When the Röntgen rays were first introduced there was one serious handicap to photography by their means—the length of the exposure. But the chemist and the scientist speedily removed this adverse factor, and now X-ray photographs can be taken instantaneously—60 per minute.

Long before this achievement Radio-photography had been yoked with the moving pictures. It was a difficult problem, but it was solved. One scientific inventor stands out prominently in this connection. This is Monsieur M. J. Carvallo who, during his position as sub-director and secretary of the Marey Institute, spared no effort to harness the X-rays to cinematography. Another illustrious worker is Dr. J. Comandon,

L 2

who may be said to be the pioneer of the
popularisation of cinematographic science.   It
was he who first appealed to the public with
films of this character under the auspices of the
well-known firm of Pathé Frères.   He has been
responsible for the preparation of many most
interesting films.   Both of these workers have
shown what can be achieved in this direction,
while the fact that they proceed upon totally
different lines adds value to their work.   It
enables their followers to decide for themselves
which principle is likely to produce the most
satisfactory result in each case.

Strictly speaking, Monsieur Carvallo's methods
would appeal more strongly to the scientific
mind, bent upon the discovery of some abstruse
phenomena, and indifferent to the complicated
process involved.   The methods of Dr. Comandon,
on the other hand, from their enhanced simplicity,
will attract the average worker.   This investigator makes a special point of accomplishing his
end in as simple a manner as possible.

From this it will be judged that radio-cinematography may be expensive or inexpensive.   This
is a correct assumption, but the amateur investigator need not fear that the deeper researches
are beyond his reach.   In justice to Monsieur
Carvallo, it must be mentioned that his experiments were undertaken at a time when radio-

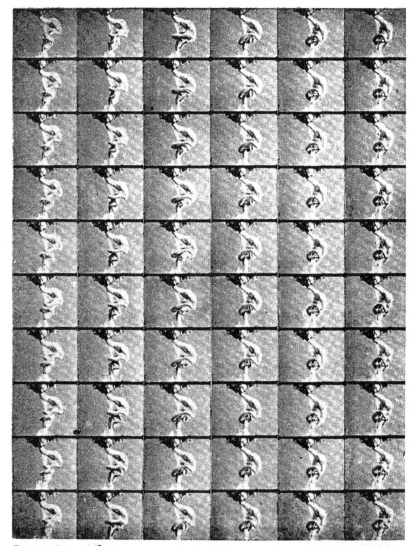

A WONDERFUL X-RAY FILM MADE BY M. J. CARVALLO.

The process of digestion in the intestine of a frog after its removal from the body.

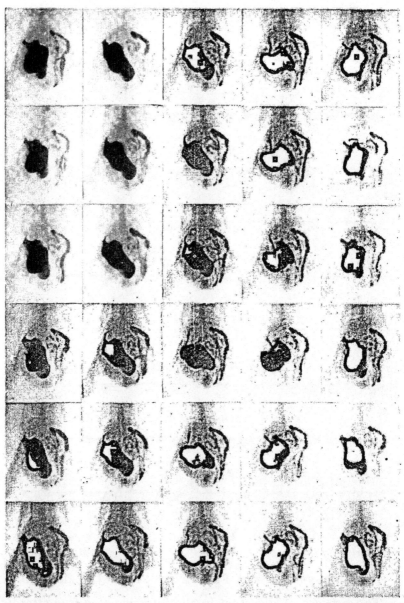

MOVING X-RAY PICTURES OF THE DIGESTION OF A FOWL.

These pictures, taken at five per second by M. J. Carvallo, show the different phases in a complete cycle of the gizzard, which lasts exactly five seconds.

photography had not reached its present stage, and therefore he had to contend with certain difficulties which no longer exist.

Monsieur Carvallo was probably the first worker to attempt to portray in movement the elusive and peculiar features revealed by the Röntgen rays. One or two other scientists had dabbled in the art, but their achievements were not very convincing for the simple reason that they did not employ chronophotography. Monsieur Carvallo, however, being fully aware of the valuable work that had been carried out by Dr. E. J. Marey, saw the true way of applying radiography to cinematography, and saw that it could not fail to be of scientific value. He embarked upon a number of illuminating, though tedious, experiments, in the effort to combine these two branches of photography.

Carvallo's installation was of a most elaborate character, but he accomplished some marvellous results, the full significance of which are appreciated only to-day. The complete apparatus he used in his experiments is shown in Fig. 9. The source of energy was a small electric motor, capable of making 2,000 revolutions per minute with a current of only 50 volts. This motor was extremely sensitive, since it would make 300 revolutions per minute with a current of 10 volts. The control of the speed was essential to his work, so he elaborated a simple and ingenious change-speed gear mechanism, which enabled him to drive the camera at four different speeds without touching the motor. The gear mechanism was not dissimilar from that adopted upon a larger scale in automobiles, lathes, and other machinery where the speed has to be varied according to the character of the work. The direct drive was transmitted from the motor-shaft to that of the camera mechanism through a belt and pulleys so as to secure flexibility and immunity from shocks. The three lower speeds were transmitted through gear wheels. These sets of wheels were mounted upon two parallel shafts and worked upon the sliding principle, which was found to be the simplest and most effective. In order to reduce the noise arising from the meshing and working of the gears the smaller wheels were made of fibre.

By this gearing system it was possible to vary the speed of the camera from 30 revolutions per second to one turn in 15 seconds. When still slower speeds were desired, upon the one-turn-one-picture principle, the motor was cut in and cut out intermittently so that the exposure could be varied from once in 20 seconds to once in an hour or more. Of course, in those instances where the exposures only needed to be made at

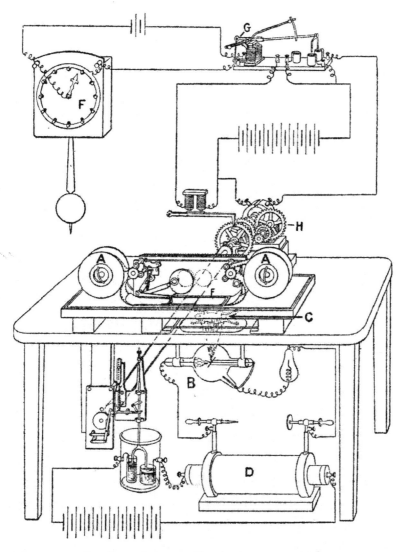

Fɪɢ. 9.—The ingenious radio-cinematographic apparatus devised by Monsieur M. J. Carvallo.

A.A. Film spools. B. Crookes tube. C. Frog being radiographed. D. Coil. ꜰ. Film. F. Clock. G. Exposure interrupter. H. Change-speed gears.

relatively prolonged intervals, the driving motor was started up intermittently so as to move the shutter at the required moment. A pendulum clock was introduced into the electrical circuit, together with a novel relay. The clock-face was provided with a ring around the dial, with the hour intervals represented by contacts instead of figures. The clock was fitted with one hand only. One electrical lead was connected to the contact ring and the other to the pivoted end of the clock-hand. When the latter came against one of the contacts the electrical circuit was completed, the motor was set in motion, and the camera mechanism was given one turn—sufficient to make an exposure and to jerk the film forward the desired distance through the gate for the next exposure. Obviously this clock system is capable of variation as desired. The contacts may be disposed to coincide with intervals of a second, a minute, an hour, or more between successive exposures. It was necessary to ensure that the contact was of sufficient duration to complete the cycle of camera movements, and, on the other hand, to prevent the motor movement being so prolonged that more than the requisite exposure and movement of the film would be made. This was effected by means of a brake, which arrested the movement of the motor after the exposure had been completed.

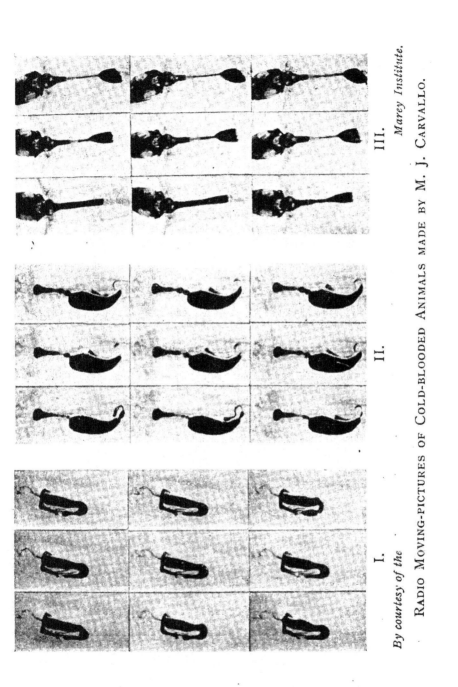

I. II. III.

RADIO MOVING-PICTURES OF COLD-BLOODED ANIMALS MADE BY M. J. CARVALLO.

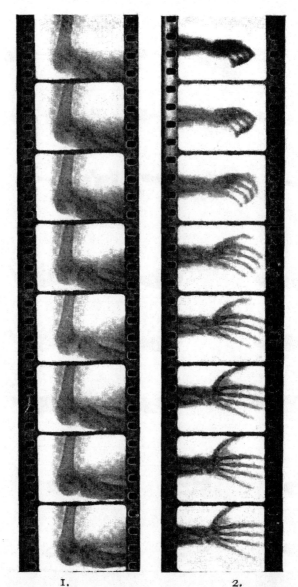

1.   2.

By permission of   *Pathé Frères.*

TWO OF DR. J. COMANDON'S EARLIEST INVESTIGA-
TIONS IN RADIO-CINEMATOGRAPHY.

1. X-ray moving-pictures of the bending of the
knee, showing muscular movement. 2. X-ray film
of the opening of the hand.

With this seemingly complicated apparatus it was possible to take any desired number of successive pictures and at any intervals of time with unerring precision.

For these particular experiments a special film was prepared, for the pictures produced by the standard camera were not large enough. Monsieur Carvallo took pictures of a depth of $2\frac{2}{5}$ inches instead of the usual $\frac{3}{4}$ inch. Special arrangements were made also to secure extreme sensitiveness of the emulsion so that it might be more susceptible to the action of the X-rays. The disposition of the film followed special lines, as may be seen by reference to the diagram (Fig. 9). The Crookes tube, containing the X-rays, was placed beneath a table provided with an aperture upon which was laid a transparent medium, such as glass, to support the subject under investigation. Above this was placed the gate through which the film was moved intermittently, the sensitized ribbon travelling in a horizontal direction from one spool to the other. In the early experiments a Maltese cross movement was incorporated to provide the requisite intermittent motion to the film, but subsequently a novel claw motion devised by Monsieur Noguès, the mechanician to the Marey Institute, was introduced with far better results.

In carrying out the experiments with different live subjects extreme ingenuity was used in placing and holding the creature so that the most perfect images might be obtained. Monsieur Carvallo devoted his energies largely to radio-cinematographing the functions of digestion, and selected such subjects as fresh-water fish, toads, frogs, lizards, birds, and mice. Thus he obtained comparative results from five species of the animal kingdom. The subjects were fed first with a special diet, comprising a mixture of flour, sugar, peptone, sub-nitrate of bismuth, and water or milk. The chemical, sub-nitrate of bismuth, was used in order to give the alimentary canal the necessary opacity to secure the best results under the Röntgen rays. In the case of the trout the chemical was injected into the blood.

In order to obtain sharp, clear, and distinct pictures upon the film, the subject under study had to be fixed in an immovable position. In the case of a trout a small celluloid envelope was made, fitted at each end with a small glass tube through which water necessary to the fish's existence was passed in a continuous stream. This vessel was only just large enough to contain the fish, so that movement was quite impossible. The top of the vessel was closed with a sheet of paraffin paper, which was placed in front of the aperture of the film gate. It was a very novel and successful means of radio-cinemato-graphing a fish under natural conditions. The fish themselves appeared to suffer no ill-effects from the method adopted to keep them alive, a trout in one instance being kept in this confined position for two consecutive days. So long as an adequate supply of fresh water was passed through the celluloid vessel in which it was encased it experienced no trouble in respiration.

In the case of the toad and frog the subject was kept in a prone position by attaching thin ribbons to the legs and extending the latter to their utmost so that the digestive organs might be radiographed clearly, distinctly, and without difficulty. The lizard, which is very difficult to photograph, was secured in a similar manner. The birds likewise were attached by their legs, and had their wings extended so that the body came directly in the path of the rays. When young birds were under investigation it was necessary to maintain a circulation of warm water around their bodies so that the tempera-ture might remain constant; otherwise the digestive functions might have been disturbed, thereby invalidating the value of the pictures. In one investigation a fowl was placed in a plaster cast so as to hold it perfectly still and steady.

The photographic speed was varied according to the character of the investigation and the subject. Thus, in recording the digestion in the stomach and intestine of the trout, an exposure was made every twenty seconds. In the case of the toad the speed was one in every ten seconds, while the chicken required one in every five.

One of the most novel experiments which Monsieur Carvallo carried out in this particular field was to ascertain the extent to which digestion will continue in the intestine after it is removed from the animal. The digestive tube of the frog was selected for this novel investigation and the photographs taken at the rate of one per second illustrate the fact that the digestive organ will continue its functions long after its removal from the body.

Since the year 1900 when Monsieur Carvallo carried out his scientific researches with the Röntgen rays, radiographic science has made great strides. Researches of this character no longer require elaborate and expensive apparatus. This has been shown by Dr. J. Comandon, the well-known French scientist, who, at the laboratories of Messrs. Pathé Frères, has prepared some magnificent X-ray films in such a manner as to make them interesting to the average patron of the picture palace. Dr. Comandon possesses the unique ability of so treating his subject as to make it appeal to the unscientific mind.

In his system Dr. Comandon does not radio-cinematograph directly in the manner of Monsieur Carvallo, but has recourse to the fluorescent screen, thereby obtaining his results much more simply and easily. By this means, also, he is able to use the standard cinematograph

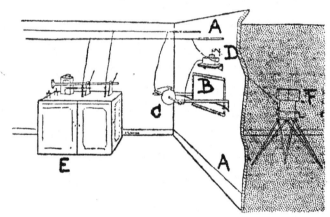

FIG. 10.—Dr. Comandon's radio-cinematographic apparatus.

camera and film without any modifications, the images upon the sensitized celluloid ribbon being of the normal size. The general arrangement of the apparatus used by this investigator is shown in the diagram (Fig. 10). A room is divided by a partition A. On one side is placed a camera F of the conventional type. On the other is the necessary electrical apparatus. An aperture B is provided in the partition, and this space is filled with a fluorescent screen. On one side of the partition A centrally in regard to the fluorescent screen, and a little distance therefrom, is placed the Crookes tube C, the subject under investigation being placed between the tube and the screen. Consequently, the radiograph is projected upon the fluorescent screen and this image is then photographed by the camera. At the normal photographing speed the exposure is about $\frac{1}{32}$ second.

The fluorescent screen employed by Dr. Comandon is of the type known as "reinforced." It is covered with tungstate of calcium, instead of barium platino-cyanide. With this screen the Röntgen rays are intensified, or rather are transformed, the luminous radiation being rendered more actinic and therefore able to act more quickly upon the emulsion of bromide of silver with which the film is coated. By using this fluorescent screen the exposure is reduced to about one-tenth of what would be required were the subject radiographed direct.

The high tension current is supplied from an apparatus of a special type E with which a current as high as 100,000 volts can be obtained. Another prominent feature is the high tension interrupter D, which cuts the electric circuit of the tube in and out, in synchrony with the camera mechanism. Thus the Crookes tube is active while the shutter is open but inactive while it is closed.

This interrupter consists of a small glass vessel, charged with petrol, and sealed with a cover of insulating material. Within the vessel, and spaced about 2 inches apart, are two brackets, which extend through the sides of the receptacle through hermetically sealed joints. To these brackets the positive and negative wires are coupled. Above the brackets, and moving within the vessel, is an inverted U-shaped piece. This slides up and down through apertures provided for the purpose in the insulated cover. When lowered to its full extent the arms rest upon the brackets, to which the wires are attached, and this contact completes the electrical circuit. A pulley wire is fixed to the centre of the inverted U-piece to allow it to be moved up and down as required. The up-and-down movement serves as a make-and-break for the circuit. A lift of a quarter of an inch suffices to break the circuit, which lift is effected by the mechanism of the camera over a system of cords and pulleys. Thus, when the camera handle is turned to open the shutter, the contact piece in the interrupter is lowered, the circuit is completed, and the Crookes tube is brought into use. Directly the shutter is closed the contact piece is raised and the tube is disconnected. This simple control permits the exposure to be varied from five or six to sixteen exposures per second, while the tube can be kept continuously at work for as many as fifty-five seconds if desired.

The camera is fitted with a lens made from quartz, which permits the maximum quantity of the actinic rays to pass through to the sensitized film. The film is covered with an exceptionally sensitive emulsion in order to ensure the best results possible with very short exposures. In order to protect the spools of film in the camera from the actinic properties of the rays diffused from the fluorescent screen, the boxes are covered with sheet lead, while the operator is protected with a lead apron, such as is used generally in Röntgen ray investigations.

The many interesting films which Dr. Comandon has produced offer adequate testimony to the practicability and success of the system which he has evolved. Undoubtedly it is the simplest and most inexpensive method of "radio-cinematography" which has been brought into practical operation up to the present, and it is one which may be followed by the private investigator with such modifications as may suggest themselves in particular cases.

CHAPTER XIII

COMBINING THE MICROSCOPE AND THE ULTRA-
MICROSCOPE WITH THE MOVING - PICTURE
CAMERA

ONE of the most fascinating fields in the whole realm of animated photography is the filming of the infinitely small by the aid of the microscope. In this manner it is possible to catch glimpses of bacterial and microbic life in natural movement, and to throw them upon the screen, where the extreme magnification enables one to follow with ease the motions of a living world invisible to the naked eye. Furthermore, the representation upon the screen is clearer, brighter, more detailed, and easier to follow, than any image seen directly through the microscope. There is an absence of that distortion and unnatural motion which often occur when the microscope alone is used.

Micro-cinematography may be either costly or cheap. As the operator in a well-equipped laboratory is able to use a camera costing £100 ($500), it is only natural to suppose that he will also be able to command the services of the most expensive type of microscope. On the other hand, the independent worker, forced by circumstances to be content with an inexpensive camera, will have to do the best he can with an inexpensive microscope also. Yet the investigator of each class can accomplish excellent work in his own sphere. I have seen some very fine films of microscopic subjects which were taken with an instrument costing less than a sovereign. From the general point of view they compared very favourably with those obtained with an instrument twenty times as costly. So long as the amateur does not attempt to embark upon work which is beyond the capacity of his microscope, and is content to work with subjects of relatively large size, there is no reason why he should not be able to take most interesting pictures.

In the preparation of micro-cinematographic subjects it is essential that the instruments should be mounted upon a solid base, a heavy bench or table, so that vibrations may be as slight as possible. The camera may be turned by hand or driven by an electric motor through belts and pulleys.

The method of mounting the microscope in its relation to the camera may be varied according to circumstances. In the simplest form the microscope is mounted horizontally with the stage on which the subject is placed set vertically, the subject itself being in line with the middle of the cinematograph lens.

In working with the microscope it must be remembered that the objects are seen by transparence. That is to say, the ray of light passes directly through, or around, the object, causing it to stand out darkly upon a luminous background. From this arises one of the limitations of the microscope. If the subjects themselves are wholly or nearly transparent, they become wholly or nearly indistinguishable in the illuminated field in which they are placed. In still-life microscopical study this disadvantage is overcome by colouring the glass slide on which the subjects are deposited, but in cinematography this operation is ruinous to the work for the simple reason that the aniline dye used to colour the slide kills the microbe whose life and movements are to be observed.

It must not be forgotten that very small organisms, as a rule, move at a speed which is quite disproportionate to their size. Some will dart hither and thither across the field of the microscope with the speed of lightning, while others will move with great deliberation. In the first case a photographing speed of sixteen pictures per second will scarcely suffice to give a faithful record of movement. The result will be a series of disconnected jumps. On the other hand, if the object moves slowly, a photographing speed of sixteen pictures per second may be too rapid. In this event the phase of movement between two successive pictures will be so slight that the projection on the screen will appear tame unless the express object is to indicate the slowness with which the organism moves. And indeed this object can be achieved with almost equally good results by taking the pictures at a slower speed, say eight, four, or even two images per second, and thus saving a good deal of film.

In most cases the micro-cinematographer works in a state of ignorance. He does not know whether he is obtaining a good or a bad film. His subject may be moving, or it may be quiescent, or it may hover round the extreme edge of the luminous field, in which case the pictures will be useless. When Mr. James Williamson and Dr. Spitta were engaged on micro-cinematograph studies some years ago, they introduced a means of following the subject through a second tube, and in this way were able to make certain that the camera was working only during those periods when the subject was in full activity, near the centre of the picture. In this way a considerable saving in film was effected.

Another difficulty is the selection and control of the light. Attempts have been made to

MICRO-CINEMATOGRAPH USED AT THE MAREY INSTITUTE FOR INVESTI-
GATING MINUTE AQUATIC LIFE.

A. One turn one picture control mechanism. B. Camera. C. Microscope. P. Small tank in which organism is placed, through which a
stream of water from tank F runs continually. E. Incandescent gas
jet for illuminating object.

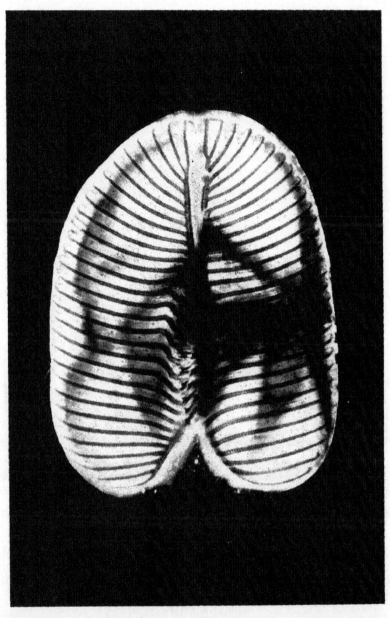

MICRO-CINEMATOGRAPHY THE PROBOSCIS OF THE BLOW-FLY.

concentrate solar light by means of a parabolic reflector or lens, and then to throw it through the microscope slide. The great drawback to this system is that intense heat is thrown upon the slide containing the organisms, and for these small creatures heat spells death. The same difficulties arise with acetylene and electric light. What is necessary is either to extinguish the light at intervals, in synchrony with the closing of the lens, or to intercept it so as to keep it off the subject until the exposure is to be made. This is done in a variety of ways by different workers.

Some years ago, when Messrs. Bull and Pizon of the Marey Institute were engaged in the micro-cinema study of a colony of marine organisms, they adopted the apparatus and method of arrangement shown in the illustration facing p. 164. The microscope C was attached to the cinematograph B which was driven by the clock A. In this case it was only necessary to make exposures at relatively long intervals, and to continue them through several days and nights, so as to obtain a complete cycle of the phases of the development of the organisms. Consequently the clock was introduced in order to make the exposures at the right intervals.

The organisms were placed in a small flat glass tank or vessel D, and were illuminated by the light from an incandescent gas burner. As it was unnecessary to keep the burner alight during the periods when the shutter was closed, Messrs. Bull and Pizon introduced a means of turning the light up and down. This was effected by a small electric magnet, working in synchrony with the clock and controlling the light so that the subject was illuminated only during exposure.

As the studies were prolonged it was essential that the water in which the organisms were placed should be kept fresh and sweet. A glass jar F was introduced to serve as a reservoir, and from this a tube extended to the vessel D. A constant flow of water was thus provided. Its circulation was ensured by another glass tube extending from the vessel P to the waste. The flow of water was controlled to a nicety by means of a tap without the production of bubbles or any other disturbance in the vessel D. In this manner the colony was preserved to the best advantage and in full activity. Some such system of circulation is necessary in all cases where the investigations are to last a long time.

In recent years the Marey Institute has much improved its micro-cinematographic apparatus. The microscope is now carried in a vertical position in front of the support which holds the camera. The camera is fitted with an external bellows which carries a prism at its outer extremity. The prism is brought over the eye-piece of the microscope. The rays of light striking the turning mirror on the base of the microscope are projected upwards through the object side or vessel and then through the eye-piece to the prism. Here the rays are bent at right angles, and are thus directed upon the travelling film in the camera. The camera is driven electrically, the motor being mounted within the box forming the base. Mechanism is introduced whereby the number of photographs per second may be varied within wide limits.

The most interesting feature of this apparatus is the means adopted to enable the worker to follow the movements of the object so that the camera can be stopped when they are of no moment or are not sufficiently near the centre of the picture. A small proportion of the light rays which have passed through the microscope are deflected from the prism mounted upon the eye-piece and thrown into a small view finder beside the camera. Looking into this view finder one can see exactly what is happening upon the stage of the microscope. This novel attachment enables the waste of film to be reduced to almost nothing.

The character of the illuminant also can be varied. Sunlight may be caught by the mirror of the microscope and projected through the instrument as well as the beam from an electric light, incandescent gas burner, or what not. With this effective and compact apparatus many marvellous microscopic experiments have been carried out at the Institute, such as the filming of the heart-beats of minute insects, and so forth. One very fascinating investigation was that carried out by Dr. J. Ries, of Switzerland, whereby he secured a cinematographic record of the different phases of the union of the sperm and the egg, as well as the separation of the membrane and segmentation of the sea urchin. The difficulties of such a delicate study were extreme, but the films obtained were of the utmost interest. They enabled the investigator to reconstruct upon the screen the complete phenomenon of fecundation. For this study the subject had to be photographed while immersed in a small vessel containing artificially prepared sea-water, which was renewed as required. The clock control enabled the camera mechanism to be so turned as to secure a regular series of exposures at the rate of seven per minute.

When Dr. Jean Comandon set himself to cinematograph the most minute microbes, which are so small that two million may be found in a cube measuring only one-twenty-fifth of an inch, he appreciated the limitations of the ordinary microscope, and the impossibility of obtaining images clearly and distinctly therewith. So he resorted to the ultra-microscope. With this instrument the light is not thrown directly through the slide containing the object, but is directed upon it by reflection from a light which stands at one side. Beneath the object to be examined is placed a glass prism, or condenser, set at right angles to the optical axis of the microscope, the result being that the light enters the slide through the edge. The objects under examination, instead of appearing as dark objects against a luminous ground as in the direct transmission of the light, appear luminous in themselves and stand out as bright spots against a dark background. By the aid of this instrument, particles which are beyond the scope of vision with the highest powered microscopes may be seen with ease.

Thus this French investigator was able to photograph even the most minute organisms. The well-known firm of Pathé Frères placed their laboratory and resources at his disposal, so that the work might be done under the most favourable conditions. Even then two years passed before a successful detailed film was obtained, and an apparatus made perfect for this class of work.

The complete apparatus is set upon a massive bench, so as to secure absolute rigidity, because vibrations are fatal to good results. Slight modifications are sometimes needed, but in most cases the same appliances are used, and in the same way. The light is furnished from a 30-ampère electric arc lamp. In front of this is arranged a series of lenses for concentrating and varying the rays, while all excess of luminosity is cut off from the microscope by means of a diaphragm. The microscope itself is set horizontally, with its longitudinal optical axis in line with that of the camera, and its eye-piece brought against the camera lens. The camera is one of the Pathé models with detachable dark-boxes.

The ray of light thrown from the electric lamp is concentrated and then falls upon the microscope condenser, which deflects it so that the objects under study become illuminated, no light entering the tube of the microscope. The camera may be turned by hand, or by a small electric motor, the latter giving an improved rotary motion with the least possible vibration.

One of the difficulties which harassed all the early efforts in micro-cinematography was the control of the light so that the subjects might not be killed by the heat generated by the concentrated rays. At first an investigation could not be continued for more than a second or two, because the microbes were killed by the heat. Seeing that the pictures were taken at the rate

THE MICRO-CINEMATOGRAPH USED AT THE MAREY INSTITUTE.

A. Special condenser. B. Electric arc light. C. Camera. D. Shutter between light and object. M. Microscope. O. Object under examination.

By permission of *Pathé Frères.*

ONE OF DR. COMANDON'S GALVANIC
EXPERIMENTS WITH PARAMŒCIA.

Under the action of electric current
the organisms perform strange evolutions.

of sixteen per second, an intermittent lighting system in synchrony with the opening of the lens was difficult to obtain, as there was the risk that the maximum illumination might not be thrown upon the subject at the precise fraction of a second during which the lens was open. Many ingenious expedients were tested to remove this disability, but without success, until at last Dr. Comandon conceived the idea of introducing a rotary shutter, similar to that fitted to the camera itself. This was tried, the shutter being placed between the condensers and the stage on which the objects were set up. This shutter was revolved by the same mechanism as drove the camera shutter, and was so timed that the opaque sector interrupted the ray of light at the same moment as the camera shutter eclipsed the lens. In this way the microbes were protected from the heat of the light while the lens was closed, and it was possible to keep them alive and in full activity in the slide for a considerable time. Repeated experiments suggested improvements in this shutter, and now the scientists employ one in which there are two or three opaque sectors of equal area spaced equidistantly, so that only a flash of light is thrown upon the microbes at the instant of exposure. Still further to lessen the evils of the heat a water condenser has been introduced between two of the glass condensers placed near the lamp. This is a small circular vessel like a big lens. It is filled with cold water and provided with the means to remove the ill effects of bubbling when the temperature rises to boiling point. The system is very much the same as that adopted by the Lumière Brothers when they first used the electric arc for the purpose of projection and with the same object— to protect the inflammable celluloid film from the heat radiated by the light.

With this ingenious and simplified apparatus Dr. Comandon has prepared some very remarkable films which have served to introduce the picture palace patrons as well as the scientists to phases of life about which little was formerly known. When thrown upon the screen the subject in some cases is magnified as many as fifty thousand times, so that the infinitesimal organisms stand up as large as dinner plates and their movements and structure and habits can easily be followed by the eye.

When the earliest films prepared by Dr. Comandon were shown by Dr. Dastre, of the Sorbonne, to the French Academy of Sciences, it was immediately realised that this was a new and reliable means of studying bacteria, and that many questions which heretofore had proved utterly unanswerable could now be solved with ease and precision. A little later the films were introduced to the public, and although it was feared that they would prove of only fleeting interest to the man in the street they have really interested him almost as deeply as the scientists. Good films of bacteria never fail to please a picture palace audience.

At present the preparation of these films is confined to a very small band of investigators. So far as bacteriology is concerned it is expert work, but there are many applications within the reach of the average microscopist. Cinematography has been of use in spreading the knowledge of the facts of health and hygiene, and now that there are propagandist movements on these subjects the aid of the living pictures will be more than ever appreciated.

CHAPTER XIV

MICRO-MOTION STUDY: HOW INCREASED WORKSHOP
EFFICIENCY IS OBTAINABLE WITH MOVING
PICTURES

In these days of competition it is obvious that
the establishment in which the machinery is
most efficient, the workmen most skilful, and
the labour most economically expended has the
best chance of success in its particular line of
business. These are the days of scientific
organisation and management, the value of which,
developed upon rational lines, cannot be denied.

But it has remained for the cinematograph to
indicate the true lines along which such developments should be continued. For instance, there
may be two workmen of equal skill and industry,
each of whom is given an identical job. One
completes his task in less time than the other,
although the two men are admittedly of equal
ability. They may be checked from stage to
stage by the stop-watch, but this will reveal
nothing conclusive, as the advantage from stage
to stage will fluctuate between the two. It is
only in the aggregate that the superiority of the

one over the other is seen.   The superiority may
be so slight as to be almost negligible, but the
fact that it exists is sufficient to prove that there
is something wrong somewhere.

Where is it?   How can it be detected?
Hitherto scientific management and stop-watch
methods have been found wanting.   The riddle
can be solved in one way only, as investigations
have shown, and that is by moving pictures.

This new phase of scientific management has
been evolved and perfected by Mr. Frank B.
Gilbreth, of New York, an eminent authority
upon the subject of workshop organisation.   He
has given it the title of " Micro-Motion Study."
As the name implies it concerns the investigation
of small movements by the ordinary standard
cinematograph and the time measurement of
each action.

While this particular line of study may not be
entirely new, since Marey and his contemporaries
in the study of movement indicated such a
possible application, yet Mr. Gilbreth is the
first to reduce it to a science.   Therefore he is
justly entitled to the credit of perfecting this
most important development of scientific management.

Everything depends upon the timing mechanism.   This must be of the simplest type and of
unimpeachable accuracy.   In a previous chapter

I have described the "chronoscope" which was used by Marey. Mr. Gilbreth, for the purposes of his work, has evolved a clock working upon a similar principle. This clock, fitted with one hand, is designed to make one complete revolution in six seconds. The indications on its dial are as follows: The larger divisions represent tenths of a revolution. Each of these is divided into two, thereby showing twentieths of a revolution, and these latter are further sub-divided into fifths, so that the dial is divided into one hundred parts. Each of these divisions represents the thousandth part of a minute, while the clock can be read easily to half-thousandths of a minute.

This clock, together with one of the ordinary type, is used in each investigation. Both are prominently displayed in the image so that the time interval from picture to picture may be determined exactly. The ordinary clock is necessary, as it shows the total time occupied in an operation. The special clock, on the other hand, serves for timing the different stages or motions involved in completing the task.

The principle may be utilised in a variety of ways, as has been proved at the works of the New England Butt Company of Providence, Rhode Island. The manager of this concern, Mr. J. G. Aldrich, was one of the first to recognise

MICRO-CINEMATOGRAPHY: BLOW-FLY EATING HONEY.

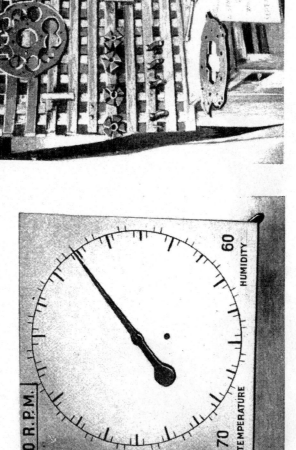

The ingenious Gilbreth clock, graduated to one-thousandths of a minute.

The rack, showing disposition of component parts for the assembling test.

MICRO-MOTION STUDY: THE LATEST DEVELOPMENT IN SCIENTIFIC MANAGEMENT.

the value and possibilities of micro-motion study.

It is an establishment devoted to the manufacture of machinery for making braiding, such as trimmings for ladies' dresses, and so forth. The machines are built for the most part from small light castings, which are machined only slightly, but which must fit together without the necessity of filing or finicking hand-work. In order to improve the efficiency of the factory and incidentally to augment its output and profit, experts were called in from time to time to say where modifications of process might reduce the manufacturing costs. Different operations in the assembling of the pieces were timed. The result was the discovery of more expeditious methods of putting the pieces together. Such time-study investigations also supplied a basis for computing the various scales and systems of payment for work done.

Notwithstanding the high pitch of efficiency to which the factory was brought by these methods, Mr. Aldrich felt convinced that still further speeding-up might be accomplished without over-driving the men. So he called in Mr. Gilbreth and his cinematographic method. In order to obtain the highest results, the most expert workman was taken as the subject of the experiment.

In one corner of the assembling room the wall and floor were marked off into four-inch squares. In this space was placed the bench, together with the sets of component parts. Here there was a slight divergence from the existing practice in the factory. Instead of taking the pieces from various boxes, packets of parts were placed in convenient positions upon a rack. These were placed in the proper sequence, so that the workman was saved the task of thinking when selecting the successive pieces. He was able to take them up quickly and correctly in a mechanical kind of way.

The timing clocks were placed in a prominent position facing the camera, and when all was ready, the workman was given the word to start. The whole operation of fitting the pieces of a machine together were filmed in this manner so as to give a complete cinematographic record of the assembling of a machine.

Now in micro-motion study the films are not intended for projection. Instead of being screened, the pictures are studied with the aid of a magnifying glass, the motion in each picture being closely examined to detect whether it is essential to the task, whether it might be eliminated, or shortened. As the wall and floor are marked off into four-inch squares, the investigator is enabled to ascertain the precise length of each movement in picking up and fitting the parts. At the same time, such marking-off enables the expert to see whether the bench and rack of packets containing the component parts of the machine are disposed most advantageously in relation to the mechanic, and also whether the latter stands in the most convenient position before his work, to fulfil his task in the shortest possible time and with the minimum of physical effort.

As might be supposed, the individual study of each picture in a film together with the following and timing of each elementary motion is a tedious task for the expert. This may be realised when it is pointed out that the time interval for each picture is only $\frac{1}{32}$ part of a second. But the labour is not wasted. The searching analysis is sure to reveal where a movement may be accelerated here, or eased there, why it would be preferable to set the rack in this position, or why it would be better if the mechanic faced his work in such and such a way. This is the sole object of micro-motion study. Nothing rivals the cinematograph for picking a movement relentlessly to pieces.

The most expert workman is taken for the purpose of the investigation because his skill must be dependent upon his ability to reduce movements to the minimum. Moreover, he serves as an excellent model for speeding-up if such is required. By the time his workmanship has been analysed and perfected by the elimination of all waste or unnecessary motions, and by his mastery of the best methods, the photographing in animation of his experience serves as a pattern for the benefit of all in the factory.

Some remarkable results have been accomplished by this new phase in scientific management. In the above-mentioned braiding factory the analysis of the movements incidental to a particular operation enabled the time occupied upon one task to be reduced from $37\frac{1}{2}$ to $8\frac{1}{2}$ minutes. In other words, the workman was able to perform more than four times his previous volume of work in an eight-hour day after his motions had been analysed by the cinematograph. Nor is he driven harder to achieve this end: he is able to do it because all waste motions have been eliminated.

The great value of micro-motion study is that it facilitates the transmission of skill from man to record. It provides a reliable way of transferring experience from a man who has gained it to one who has never had it. It acts as a check upon the work. The establishment is provided with an unassailable record of the time occupied throughout every department, and consequently holds a complete check upon the skill and capacity of every man. If there is a decrease in the output, showing slackness to exist somewhere, it can be traced before material damage is inflicted. Every workman is kept up to concert pitch, and the maximum work per man is obtained without resort to driving or rushing.

There is no limit to the applications of micro-motion study. Obviously, although the best efforts of every man are required, it is essential that the records should be taken under normal conditions, so as to provide a fair basis. To introduce special arrangements for the test is to destroy the value of the investigations, because the other men will retort that they cannot equal the performance unless they have the same facilities.

The workmen are never permitted to see the moving-picture record of their work. Neither are they shown contrasting views of how and how not to do a thing. The pictures are merely for the use of the investigator. When it is necessary to communicate the results of an experiment to the workman, he is given no opportunity for argument. He is merely told how to do this or that, according to the experience gathered from an intimate study of the photographic record.

This application of the cinematograph has been developed also for the benefit of apprentices. A

youth who is trained on the correct lines from
the very commencement of his duties has the
best chance of becoming an expert workman, and
for him the use of micro-motion study is invaluable. He can be taken through every
separate motion step by step, the film used for
this purpose being that of the most perfectly
skilled man. Experience has shown, moreover,
that a youth can learn his craft more quickly and
intelligently by following it upon the screen than
by being brought face to face with the actual
work at the bench. He appears to concentrate
his attention better upon the moving-picture
lesson than upon the practical demonstration,
although in both cases the appeal is made to the
eye.

There is yet another valuable aspect of this
work. Enterprising and ingenious men are
constantly devising improved processes in factory
equipment. At times their revolutionary ideas
are put into practice before they are thoroughly
understood, and the result is far from satisfactory.
The improvement proves to be more imaginary
than real. But if recourse is first had to the
cinematograph, the process can be submitted to a
searching practical trial before it is installed. A
film can be taken and each separate image can be
examined minutely with the aid of the magnifying
glass, until a pretty complete idea is gained as to

Mr. Frank B. Gilbreth cinematographing a man's work against time, showing the Gilbreth clock.

Bench and parts arranged after test so as to secure assembling of machine with fewest and shortest motions.

THE GILBRETH METHOD FOR IMPROVING FACTORY EFFICIENCY.

1   2

MICRO-MOTION STUDY: FILMS SHOWING HOW A MAN'S WORK IS
ANALYSED BY MOVING PICTURES.

These pictures are not thrown on the screen, but are examined by
a magnifying glass.

(1) Film of workman assembling machine, showing Gilbreth clock

the true value of the invention. The pictorial time record can be compared with the best results secured under the existing practice, and the manufacturer can ascertain what economies the new plan will effect before a penny is expended, or the working of his factory disorganised by the alteration.

Micro-motion study by the aid of the cinematograph is still in its infancy. But it appears to have a wide field of utility. The pictures can be taken at any desired speed, according to the character of the work photographed, but as a rule sixteen pictures per second will suffice. It must be remembered that in this case the record is not obtained for the purpose of studying movement from the scientific or physiological point of view, as with Marey's investigations, but purely for the purpose of discovering whether certain motions are necessary to certain tasks. Obviously the expert engaged in this work must possess an intimate knowledge of movement so as to be able to follow the motions closely and accurately through their natural cycles, and must also be familiar with the work of the factory so as to tell whether a man is working to the best advantage. This faculty alone demands a long apprenticeship, for experience is the only guide. Mr. Frank B. Gilbreth, who has brought micro-motion study prominently before the public, has devoted years

to the subject.   He has become an unique
authority upon it.   Now that its advantages are
appreciated, one may expect it to fill an even
wider space in industrial life, and to be applied in
many directions that are as yet undreamed of.

CHAPTER XV

THE MOTION PICTURE AS AN AID TO SCIENTIFIC INVESTIGATION

RAPID strides are being made in the utilisation of animated photography as an aid to scientific investigation. It is a development useful in all fields of research where phenomena can be recorded in pictorial form. Dr. E. J. Marey, the eminent French scientist, was the pioneer in this work. One has only to peruse his classic work "Movement"[1] to realise the comprehensive nature of his studies. So thoroughly did he cover the ground of chronophotography, as it was then called, that it is difficult to conceive where any new application of the motion picture can now be made.

The Aurora Borealis always has been a subject fascinating to scientists. Numerous papers and brochures have been written about it, and many elaborate drawings have been prepared to convey some idea of its characteristics and its kaleidoscopic changes. The drawings, however, fail to

[1] "Movement," by E. J. Marey. Heinemann, 7s. 6d.

convince, and even the few still-life photographs which have been taken are uneventful.

Realising this deficiency a Danish professor is striving to record the Aurora Borealis in motion upon the celluloid film. A special camera has been designed for his work, and with this it is intended to snap the phenomena from a convenient northern point such as Spitzbergen or Greenland, not only for the benefit of the scientific world but also for the general public which entertains only a hazy conception of the " Northern Lights." It need hardly be said that if this investigator should succeed in his difficult quest he will reveal upon the screen one of the most extraordinary wonders of the world. While the marvellous and weird colouring effects will be missing, the curtains of light that drape the sky, and the strange luminous shafts and glares which light the heavens, should provide a film of intense interest and fascination.

The moving-picture camera is also being applied to the recording of solar eclipses with a view to obtaining a more impressionistic and intimate idea of the activity and extent of the flames which shoot from the surface of the sun. Wonderful still-life pictures of these effects have been taken, and it is only fair to assume that they should be capable of being caught by the motion-picture camera. Efforts are also being made to

secure photographs of the heavens, but the difficulties are very great. The long exposure required in this case is a heavy drawback, but
seeing that the slowest movements of Nature
can be recorded by the cinematograph, and may
be speeded up in projection to convey the effect
of animation, there is no reason why similar
moving pictures of other worlds should not be
obtained by combining the moving-picture camera
with the telescope. The moon followed through
its phases would yield an interesting study, and,
incidentally, a film of this character would possess
considerable educational value.

At the present moment great activity is being
manifested in the application of the cinematograph
to mechanics. Two Sheffield investigators have
designed a steel-testing machine to which is
attached a microscope and a cinematograph
camera. The piece of steel to be tested is placed
in the machine and the cinematograph is set in
motion. By throwing the resulting pictures upon
the screen it is possible to follow exactly what
takes place in the molecular construction of the
steel while it is under test.

The idea has been applied to many other
phases of mechanics with equal success, and
there have been many discoveries of a technical
nature which have had their effect upon manufacturing processes.

Another series of technical experiments was carried out by Dr. Otto Füchs, professor of engineering at the German Technical High School of Brünn. The purpose was to elucidate some hitherto obscure points in connection with the working of steam hammers. Investigations in this field have hitherto proceeded on the graphic principle, the results being recorded by a stylo continually travelling over calibrated paper. It is admitted that this system leaves much to be desired because the stylo is not sufficiently sensitive, and fails to record many of the smaller and more important movements. Accordingly, Dr. Füchs conceived the idea of using the moving-picture camera in the anticipation that much missing data might thus be discovered.

A special apparatus was designed. In reality it is an ingenious combination of the moving-picture camera and the graphic method. There is a paper tape that passes continuously over two rollers and has two stylos constantly bearing on it. These stylos are connected with two indicators attached to the sides of the cylinder of the steam hammer, and they supply a continuous record of the steam pressure. The paper tape is moved by an electrically-driven gear, while time intervals are indicated by means of clockwork mechanism. So much for the graphic portion. What the cinematographic portion supplies is

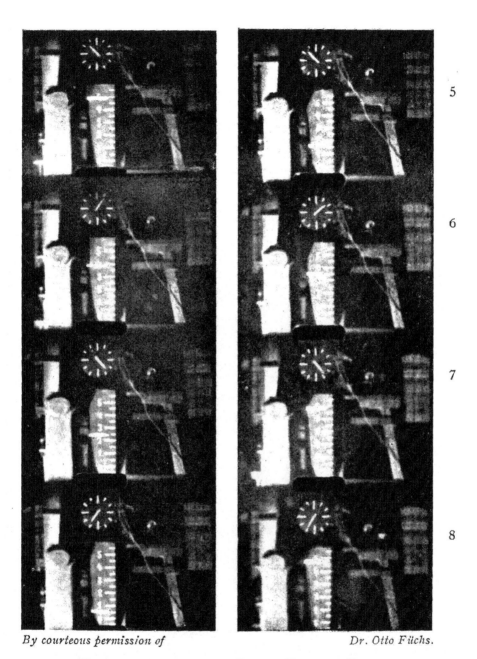

5

6

7

8

By courteous permission of   *Dr. Otto Fūchs.*

MOVING-PICTURES OF A STEAM HAMMER RAM.

An illuminated index attached to the ram moves over a graduated scale, ιile an illuminated clock indicates the lapse of time.

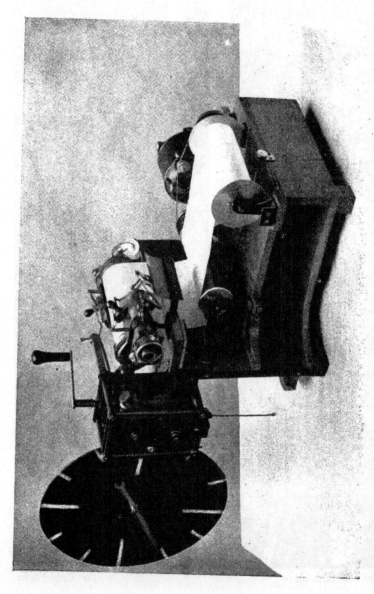

DR. OTTO FÜCHS' APPARATUS FOR TAKING MOVING-PICTURES OF THE OPERATIONS OF A STEAM HAMMER.

a continuous animated record of the movement of the ram of the hammer. Attached to the ram is an index which moves up and down over a scale divided into centimetres. Both the index and the scale are illuminated so that the result given by the camera shows a series of photographic images of the oscillating motion. Above the illuminated finger and scale is a clock similar to Marey's chronoscope and Gilbreth's timepiece, driven by clockwork, and in synchrony with the remainder of the mechanism. This scale likewise has its points of division illuminated. Its use is to supply the time factor without which such experiments are useless.

The ram, the index-finger, the scale and the clock are all recorded upon the film, so that it is possible to tell the varying speeds at which the ram moves throughout its travel. The photographing speed may be varied as desired, and as a different position is caught in each picture, the distance the ram travels between two successive exposures, together with the time occupied in completing the cycle of movement, may be accurately gauged. The combination of the paper tape recorder with the photographic part of the apparatus affords a complete record of the ram's performance.

The results are naturally of a severely technical

character and of interest only to persons concerned with mechanics. But to these they are very important indeed. The experiments which have been completed by Dr. Füchs have thrown much light upon a difficult engineering problem. They have served to answer questions affecting the design of the hammer and its most economical efficient operation which would otherwise have been insoluble. From the public point of view the films possess no interest whatever, inasmuch as the subject is illuminated and photographed in such a way that only the features of technical interest are brought out strongly upon the film.

Another interesting and profitable province of the cinematograph is that concerning ballistics. This has been worked out by Monsieur Lucien Bull at the Marey Institute with his camera capable of taking two thousand pictures per second under the illumination of the electric spark. While this investigator did not apply his invention directly to ballistics he indicated the manner in which such work could be carried out. The success of his experiments, however, prompted another investigator to enter the field. This was Dr. Cranz, of the Berlin Military Academy. The apparatus this professor evolved has been devoted exclusively to the study of the flight of projectiles and to photographing the

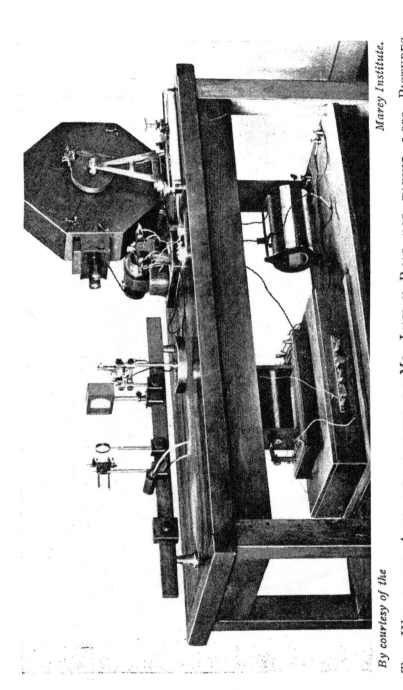

By courtesy of the

Marey Institute.

THE WONDERFUL APPARATUS DEVISED BY MR. LUCIEN BULL FOR TAKING 2,000 PICTURES
PER SECOND.

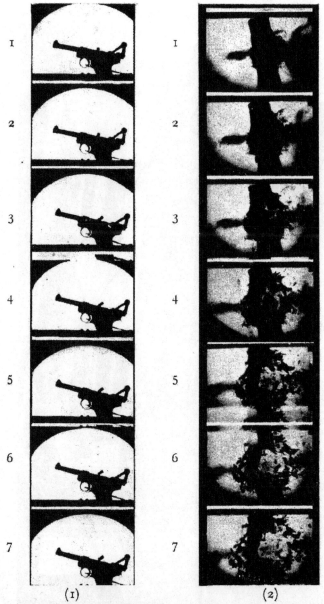

FILMS PREPARED BY PROFESSOR CRANZ WITH HIS
REMARKABLE CAMERA.

(1) Moving-pictures of the ejection of a cartridge from
an automatic pistol.

(2) Motion photographs of the splintering of a bone
by a bullet.

action of the mechanism of the magazine type of firearm.

The Cranz apparatus is somewhat more complicated than that designed by Monsieur Bull, though the fundamental principle of operation is the same. The film, resembling an endless belt, is passed round two steel cylinders, one of which is driven by an electric motor. Images of standard size are produced under the illumination of the electric spark, which concentrates the maximum amount of light upon the moving object. The photograph is in silhouette, and the disposition of the apparatus is such that five hundred consecutive pictures can be made in one-tenth of a second, the period of exposure varying between one-millionth and one-ten-millionth of a second. The outstanding feature of the installation is the special and novel type of interrupter. It consists of a pendulum by which the sparking is started before the projectile is fired and made to continue until the film has been exhausted.

Some of the results obtained by this apparatus are very remarkable. When the films are projected upon the screen at the average speed of sixteen pictures per second the flight of the bullet can be followed with ease. One film shows the effect of a bullet striking a suspended india-rubber ball filled with water, and brings out the remarkable formations the ball assumes during the infinitesimal part of a second when the bullet is passing through it. Another interesting film shows the effect of a high velocity bullet striking a bone, and the manner in which the bone is splintered and smashed by the force of the impact conveys a realistic impression of the destructive force of the modern rifle projectile. The deadliness of the automatic pistol is well known. Since seven shots may be discharged in four seconds, the movements of the mechanism are too rapid to be followed by the naked eye. Yet by means of the Cranz apparatus every motion is caught, and the whole is slowed down in projection to such a degree that the complete cycle of the firing of the shot and the expulsion of the cartridge, which normally occupies only a fraction of a second to complete, occupies about thirty seconds upon the screen. When these pictures were exhibited for the first time a number of black specks were observed to accompany the expulsion of the spent cartridge. These proved to be grains of powder which had not been ignited. Their existence had never before been suspected, and the result was curious. After minute examination of the pictures a change was effected in manufacture of the cartridge so that the waste of powder through non-ignition should be reduced to the minimum. The success achieved in this direction was shown by the absence of non-ignited grains in subsequent pictures.

Another wonderful series of moving pictures was prepared by an American ophthalmic surgeon. He embarked upon elaborate researches to gain further information about the eye and its peculiarities both in sickness and in health. The illumination of the eye was carried out very cleverly, so as to obtain the greatest possible brilliancy without causing fatigue to the subject. Accordingly his pictures were absolutely normal. In these experiments glass plates were used, for the reason that they give results much finer and more detailed than celluloid. In celluloid the grain of the base of the film is apt to be disturbing to very fine studies. In this way a great deal of new information was gained. One of the most remarkable discoveries was that the sensitiveness of the organ of sight is far greater than was previously supposed, and that the eye never is absolutely still, even when commonly regarded as being fixed and steady.

During the past two or three years the uses of the cinematograph in medicine have been much extended. A former chapter has described its application to the study of microbic life, but the latest innovation is to employ it in the operating room.

The pages of the medical papers are filled with reports of curious and unusual surgical operations, but mere reports are necessarily somewhat imperfect. In view of these circumstances it occurred to one eminent surgeon that a cinematographic record would form a first-class supplement to the technical description. The initial experiment proved a complete success, and accordingly the practice has been extended. In this direction France, Germany, and the United States are taking a very active part. Films of this character can be made to serve two useful purposes. They are valuable for the transmission of practical information between medical men and are useful in the lecture room among the students. Suppose a hospital in New York has a strange and unusual case for operation. Only the students in that establishment have the opportunity of witnessing it. But by the aid of the moving-picture camera and a lecture it can be reproduced in photographic animation upon the screen for the benefit of medical graduates in the various hospitals throughout the world.

In research work, such as the study of new and unusual diseases, especially those of a tropical nature, it is possible to obtain a continuous record of a subject from the moment of infection through the various stages of the malady. For instance, in the study of sleeping sickness in Uganda, Colonel Bruce had formerly to content himself with a graphic record or chart of the fluctuations of a patient's condition, with explanatory notes introduced here and there when a sudden change in the temperature or general behaviour of the patient developed. With the cinematograph it is possible to obtain a pictorial record which conveys a more forceful and exact impression of the symptoms. An interesting indication of what could be done in this direction was the film prepared by Dr. Comandon. He used a monkey for his subject, infecting it with the microbe of sleeping sickness discovered by Colonel Bruce. The effects which the bacteria produced upon the monkey were admirably illustrated, together with the changes that various remedies wrought in its condition.

So far as concerns the application of the cinematograph to scientific research the greatest strides have been made in physiology. This was due to Marey's enthusiasm in this branch of science, and the establishment of the Physiological Institute in Paris where such investigations were carried out upon a most exhaustive scale. The results of Marey's investigations are given in several volumes and in hundreds of papers which he sent to the various French scientific societies. There is no reason why the contributions of the cinematograph to physiological knowledge should not be equalled in other branches of science. Up to the present the investigation of scientific phenomena with the aid of motion-pictures has not been carried far, but there are many signs that its sphere will be extended in the future.

CHAPTER XVI

THE MILITARY VALUE OF THE CINEMATOGRAPH

AMONG the many uses of the cinematograph, frivolous and useful, amusing and instructive, perhaps none has proved so difficult or illusive as the attempt to apply it to soldiering for the purpose of improving marksmanship. The motion-picture had scarely impressed itself upon the public when the war departments of the various powers were flooded with suggestions and patents for its employment in this sphere. Needless to say the majority of these ideas were found to be impracticable, and probably this is the reason why the animated target has not been seriously taken up by military authorities.

Notwithstanding the many disabilities under which the cinematograph labours, it is generally admitted that it has real practical value in this field up to a certain point. It is able to induce the recruit to aim quickly and surely, and this is to-day recognised as being the governing consideration whether the range be point-blank or long-distance.

One of the first practical developments in this direction was that perfected by Messrs. Paterson and Musgrave.   Their wide and diversified experience of all that pertains to shooting and targets enabled them to avoid the defects of the system, which to many experimenters were not apparent owing to a lack of knowledge.

The apparatus and method of operation were very simple.   The target consisted of an endless roll of white paper which served as the screen, and upon which the pictures were projected from a point near the firing line.   A self-recording system was incorporated whereby the result of a shot was transmitted back to the firing line to inform the marksman about the value of his hit. As the paper became perforated under the fusilade it was rolled up.   The most important feature of this invention was the mechanism placed behind the screen, which synchronised with the movements of the objects at which the marksman aimed.

In cinematographic projection, however, the throw of the picture cannot be extended beyond certain limits, that is, if a clear view is to be presented to those seated farthest away from the screen.   In target practice this is a serious disadvantage.   At a range of 200 feet marksmanship would be almost impossible, owing to the indistinctness of the image upon the white wall.

At that distance one always receives an impression of flicker. Why this should be so is not quite apparent, though it is evidently governed by some law of optics. Suppose, for instance, that a picture is being followed from a distance of 200 feet, and a straining of the eyes is experienced. This may be overcome merely by looking at the screen through the reverse end of a pair of field glasses. As is well known, this usually makes the object appear to recede to a great distance, but when it is done in connection with moving pictures it makes the images stand out more brilliantly and distinctly, while they are far steadier, the flickering being almost entirely eliminated. In fact, if one wishes to witness a projection to the best advantage with the minimum of eye fatigue, this is the way to do it.

It is obvious, under these circumstances, that the distance of the marksman from the target is restricted somewhat severely. From 75 to 100 feet is considered to be the greatest distance from which shooting can be practised to advantage. Since the modern automatic pistol will carry about 80 yards, while the latest types of rifles have a range of 1,000 yards or more, doubts may be raised as to the utility of the cinematograph in marksmanship. In the Paterson-Musgrave invention an ingenious attempt to overcome this disability was made by what

might be termed a "range compensation." This
end was achieved by making the figures of
varying sizes, according to their distance from
the marksman, so that a target of varying size
was presented. Thus in one case the man would
appear in the foreground of the picture and be of
relatively large size, corresponding to the target
he would offer at a distance of 100 yards. Then
he would be shown somewhat smaller to represent
500 yards, and so on, until at the higher distances
he offered a very small target indeed.

From the military point of view the incidents
were made as exciting as possible, and closely
analogous to actual war conditions. As a case in
point, the man on the screen would be shown
behind cover, and aiming directly at the man on
the firing line. His movements could easily be
followed. He would be seen to expose himself
slightly to sight his rifle and then to fire. The
effect upon the marksman firing at the target was
thrilling in its apparent realism, because he unconsciously developed the feeling that he had got
to shoot first, and straight, or he would be hit.
The self-recording system enabled him to judge
whether he had got his shot well home, while the
judge could decide whether the marksman or
the photographic enemy had fired first.

The judicious selection of subjects for portrayal
upon the screen undoubtedly served to develop

a sense of smartness among the marksmen. A decided improvement in quick-sighting or snap-shooting was obtained together with a concentration upon the work in hand.

Projection was carried out upon purely automatic lines. The projector was set working by a button control placed at the firing point, and pressed by the marksman or his officer. The instructor or officer had thus a complete control over the whole installation, and was in a position to make sure that his instructions were being followed, as well as being able to tell whether his men were quick in sighting. Despite the many ingenious features incorporated in this idea, it does not appear to have met with official approval.

There has recently been another invention, based upon a similar idea. This is what is called the "Life Target," and it is ingenious, practical, and well thought out, especially from the mechanical and electrical points of view. The original idea was suggested by a non-commissioned Irish officer who fought through the Boer war. His suggestion in its crude form, however, was scarcely feasible, but there were three other patents available, each of which had been designed for a different purpose, and it was realised that a combination of the four would enable a practicable cinematographic target to be produced. Even then, innumerable experiments were required before perfection was gained.

In this invention the salient feature is that when a shot is fired at the screen the whole of the mechanism is stopped for a very brief period, and the hit is indicated by a bright spot of light on the target. Consequently the marksman is able to ascertain instantly the effect of his shot, and has no need to remove his eye from the object at which he has aimed. This is a distinct advantage, because the marksman can keep his sight ready for the succeeding shot, which may be fired instantly the mechanism resumes working. Directly the film begins to move once more the previous shot represented by the illuminated spot upon the target is extinguished.

The apparatus, as described, appears to be rather complicated, but as a matter of fact its working is extremely simple. The projector is mounted at a convenient place near the firing point, so that a truly square picture is presented to the marksman. In front of the firing line, and above the picture, is a very sensitive microphone or telephone receiver. Connected with this is a delicate relay, which really forms the heart of the mechanism.

When a shot is fired the report acts upon the microphone and upon the relay in turn.

Immediately a magnetic clutch, which is placed upon the motor drive of the projector, is released, and a brake arrests the movement of the projector mechanism. Thus, the passage of the film is stopped in the gate, so that the picture remains stationary upon the screen.

The screen itself consists of three separate sheets of specially prepared thick paper. The front sheet is coiled upon a horizontal roller which is mounted at the bottom. From this it is carried up and over a second horizontal roller at the top of the screen space, and then down again behind the front sheet, to be coiled upon a third horizontal roller, mounted above the first one. As the lower front roller can be moved or "fed" the paper is free to travel upwards over the top roller, and down again to be wound upon the third roller. Behind these two thicknesses of vertically travelling paper is mounted a third sheet. This is coiled upon a vertical roller at one side, passed across the back of the two front sheets, and coiled round a second vertical roller on the opposite side. It is kept very taut, and serves to hold the two sheets in front in close proximity. It is moved by hand at intervals.

Behind the screen are a number of arc electric lights, or other illuminants, out of the firing line. In this way the space behind the screen is brilliantly lighted.   As the paper remains stationary while the projector is running, it follows that a shot must penetrate the three thicknesses of paper, and the puncture is shown by the light from behind coming through the shot-hole.   Thus the marksman can see where his shot has struck.

When the projecting mechanism has been stopped, and the result has been read, the shot-hole has to be obliterated before the film is able to resume its forward movement.   This is accomplished automatically as follows: The relay, while declutching the drive and applying the brake, also sets in motion a plunger in a dash-pot.   The time of the vertical travel of this plunger is varied, but the mechanism remains stationary, and the shot-hole visible, during its movement.   When it has reached the limit of its travel it establishes contacts which serve to set the screen mechanism in motion.   On the lower horizontal roller carrying the supply of paper is a ratchet and pawl movement, actuated by a solenoid.   When the plunger connected with the relay closes the screen mechanism circuit, the ratchet is moved, and the outer sheet of paper moves upward one-eighth of an inch, while its return forming the second sheet moves simultaneously and correspondingly downwards. The displacement of these two vertically moving

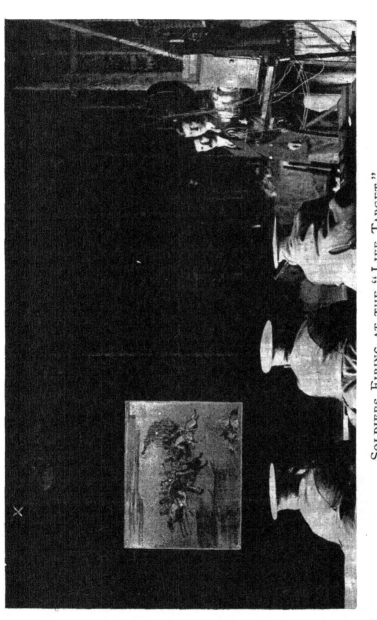

SOLDIERS FIRING AT THE "LIFE TARGET."

The picture on the screen is thrown from the projector at right, and the picture is held stationary by the action of the report of the rifle caught by the microphone (marked X) upon the lantern mechanism.

FRONT VIEW OF THE "LIFE TARGET," SHOWING SCREEN OPENING.

sheets disturbs the line of holes caused by the shot, and through which the back light was shining, so that the spot of light is extinguished, and an opaque screen is presented. The inclusion of the third or back paper not only serves as a stiffener, but also acts as a means of lessening the possibility of a repeat, especially as it is moved gradually and at long intervals in a transverse direction. The movement of the travelling surfaces of paper is extremely small, approximately the diameter of a shot-hole, so that the consumption of paper is very low. When the first roller has been exhausted it is only necessary to replace it by the roller on which the paper has been rewound, and the paper can be used over again. The possibility of three old shot-holes coming once more into line without a shot being fired is so extremely remote as not to be worth consideration.

From this it will be seen that the final stage in the cycle of movements arising from the action of the rifle report upon the microphone, and the relay, is the movement of the paper forming the screen or target. The time during which the picture remains stationary may be varied within certain limits, but normally it is about a couple of seconds. When the paper has moved, obliterating the shot-hole, the brake on the projector is released, the magnetic clutch re-engages, and the film resumes its travel. The ingenious means adopted for stopping and restarting the projector will be appreciated as a great feature of the invention, and though the action may appear to be abrupt, no damage whatever is inflicted upon the film.

One point about this apparatus deserves attention. In the ordinary projector, if the celluloid film is stopped in the gate for a fraction of a second, and is exposed to the light, it flares up instantly, owing to the great heat emitted by the illuminant and the high inflammability of the film. As it is necessary to allow the film to stand still upon the screen in this case, after the shot has been fired, means had to be found to keep it sufficiently cool to prevent combustion. This is done by a radiator arranged around the condenser, which in itself is a special kind of cooling tank.

Another noteworthy point is the way in which a still-life lantern slide is thrown upon the screen when desired. The projector carries two lenses, one for animation, and the other for still-life lantern slide work. The ordinary way of bringing the latter into use is to push the front part of the projector bodily sideways so as to bring the second lens before the condenser and the light. The objection to this method is that the rigidity of the projector is likely to be disturbed, especially after a little wear, with the result that the projection of the moving pictures is apt to become

THE SCREEN MECHANISM OF THE "LIFE TARGET."

The movement of the rollers and paper forming the screen is made by means of a solenoid operated by the lantern mechanism.

CINEMATOGRAPHING HEDGE-ROW LIFE UNDER DIFFICULTIES.

Mr. Frank Newman and his camera concealed in the scrub.

unsteady. In this apparatus a mirror is placed in the lantern and set at an angle of 45 degrees. By this means the light can be diverted and thrown through the lantern slide lens. Thus it is not only possible to throw a still-life slide upon the screen at the instant when a moving-picture scene is completed, but excellent dissolving effects can be obtained.

The pictures are projected at the normal speed, but this may be accelerated if necessary. Any films suited to the subject may be used, hydroplanes, airships, birds, wild animals, and so forth, just as successfully as the military films prepared specially for the work. In fact any picture where movement is portrayed is equally applicable, so that the marksman can become used to all sorts of conditions. Experience has shown, however, that a picture projected at the normal speed of sixteen per second is too rapid for the average man unless the object was moving slowly when photographed. It has been proved that practice with this target improves quick-sighting and so teaches the art of snap-shooting which is said to be the essence of modern marksmanship. After a little experience the marksman develops the tendency to sight instantaneously as he lifts his weapon. For training in revolver shooting, which is essentially short-range point-blank work, it would be difficult to conceive a better system.

Even if considered as a mere diversion the life target has many advantages. There is a sensational realism which is lacking in the ordinary shooting gallery. The man at the firing point is occupying the same relative position as that of the cinematographer when he filmed the subject, and when, for instance, a tiger is springing directly out of the picture, the man with the gun has just the same feeling as if caught at close quarters in the jungle. He sights and fires quickly, hoping to hit in a vital part, and the instantly appearing shot-hole tells him how he would have fared had he been face to face with the animal in its native haunts.

So far as military shooting is concerned the system has its limitations. For the reasons explained the screen cannot be more than 100 feet from the firing line. It is a pure point-blank range. No allowances can be made for windage or trajectory. There is yet another factor that controls the distance between the firing range line and the screen, and that is that paper cannot be obtained in widths exceeding 9 feet. A single width must form the screen, since no light must be visible from it until it is perforated by a bullet. So there is a strict limit to the size of the target. But it is possible to get subjects life size, and nothing more is required.

CHAPTER XVII

THE PREPARATION OF EDUCATIONAL FILMS

ALTHOUGH animated photography is regarded popularly as an amusement, and the picture palace is maintained to be the poor man's theatre, efforts are being made to lift the invention into a higher and more useful plane. It is sought to adapt it to the schoolroom, the college and the technical institute. Up to the present, however, little headway has been made in this direction, though the market is flooded with so-called educational films.

Unfortunately the attitude of the responsible authorities is lukewarm, somewhat to the chagrin of those who are specializing in the preparation of these films. The authorities are said to be prejudiced against the invention, and no doubt the impression still lingers that the cinematograph is an instrument of frivolity.

Up to a point the authorities are correct in their attitude. It is the producer who is at fault, The former recognise the many advantages arising from the appeal to the eye, but unfortunately the producer looks at the question from the show-

man's point of view. He is not content to prepare a subject which shall appeal only to pupils
as such, but is always trying to introduce an
element which shall make the film popular with
adults as well. He seeks to arouse the enthusiasm of the schoolroom and of the picture
palace at one and the same time, though the two
are as widely apart as the two poles, and what is
suited to one is by no means adapted to the other.
The patron of the picture palace must be enter-
tained only. Education, if any, must be uncon-
scious. On the other hand, the essential consideration in the school is the training and
teaching of the young mind. If amusement is
ntroduced the educational value of the film is
liable to be small.

In this attempt to supply two different markets
simultaneously many producers over-reach themselves. They fail to realise that a schoolroom
film must be absolutely natural, that there must
be no trickery or faking. There are several
films on the market to-day, aiming at the requirements of education, wherein the most attractive
incidents are nothing more nor less than examples
of fake photography. The educational authorities are only too well aware that trickery is
one of the cinematographer's most useful tools,
and accordingly many films of an apparently
astonishing character are regarded with sus-

picion.   Until all traces of faking and chicanery are abandoned the authorities are certain to look coolly on the suggestion of teaching by the cinematograph.

Nevertheless the film must be prepared in such a manner that the pupil is not bored.   It must be rendered interesting and fascinating or it will be no better than the old Dry-as-dust teaching.   And the infusion of interest is by no means difficult.   Every branch of science, every item in the curriculum, can be taught by motion pictures.   One producer has prepared a novel and interesting film for teaching the alphabet and the spelling of simple words with the aid of a troupe of acrobats.   The acrobats contort themselves into the shapes of letters upon the screen before the children's eyes.   The children naturally follow the process with interest, and the finished letter at once impresses itself upon their minds.   The spelling of the words is carried out in the same way.

Another producer has a novel idea for explaining the principles of addition, subtraction, multiplication, and division.   He has devised animated scenes with teddy bears and oranges, and the setting itself is a schoolroom.   The actors, who are children, are dressed in bear skins, and they behave in a truly grizzly manner.   The very fact that this favourite toy is introduced rivets the attention of young children, and they follow the arithmetical adventures of the oranges with the utmost fascination. The bears themselves perform their parts most decorously, without any horseplay or clowning. The youngsters following the incidents upon the screen are induced to regard the projection seriously, and it has been found that afterwards, in their leisure hours, they reconstruct the incidents with their own toys. In this way they show that they have grasped the idea that was to be conveyed.

In dealing with the sciences similar methods must be practised. Suppose, for instance, that it is intended to teach physics, chemistry, or electricity with the aid of moving-pictures. The film must commence at the very beginning of the subject. The text-book should be taken as a model. The producer of the film, if he is well acquainted with his subject, can devise experiments to suit any stage of knowledge. He can vary the experiment so as to bring the pupil face to face with something which has never been illustrated by diagram in the text-book. He can lead the pupil on step by step, and the more deeply he plunges into a particular science the wider is his scope for the portrayal of fascinating experiments.

The preparation of films of this character offer attractive possibilities to the independent worker,

(1) Moor-hen sitting on her Nest.

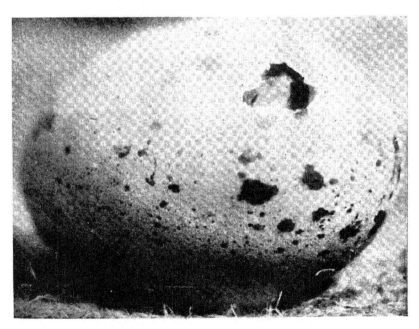

(2) The Young Chick pierces the Shell.

(3) THE CHICK EMERGING FROM THE SHELL.

(4) THE NEWLY-HATCHED CHICK STRUGGLING TO ITS FEET.

especially if he is familiar with teaching methods. The professional producer is often unable to reduce his subjects to the requisite simplicity. As a rule he knows little or nothing about a schoolroom, and the result is that he confines himself to the preparation of extremely fascinating films of a very advanced type, suited to the student in the secondary school or to one who has mastered the rudiments of the science. But it is in the laying of a solid foundation that the teacher finds his greatest difficulty. As a rule he has to go over the ground repeatedly before the elementary points sink into the pupil's mind. This drudgery can be greatly reduced by use of the moving-pictures, if only the right type of film is shown. The professional producer maintains that such an elementary film is useless, merely because he looks at it from the showman's point of view.

Another reason why the independent cinematographer should embark upon this field is that he is generally more ingenious and fertile in the preparation of experiments to suit the limitations of a lesson. He will know how to be simple, so that the pupil, after the demonstration, can go into the laboratory and repeat the experiments with a knowledge of what he is doing.

As the pupil advances the films may be varied. For instance, in the experiments with sulphur he can be shown how sulphur is obtained. Views can be introduced of the mines and processes as practised in Sicily or Louisiana, and in this case the difference between ancient and modern methods can be brought home to him. Similarly in regard to the subject of common table salt it is possible to show the various methods of extraction, from the solar evaporating system practised in the Caucasus and California, and the excavation of rock salt as in Galicia, to the pumping of brine and forced evaporation common to the " Wiches " of England. The film may be " lightened " by glimpses of bathing in the Great Salt Lake or the brine baths of England in order to convey pictorially the difference in the density of salt and fresh water. In many cases it is possible to reproduce upon the screen the processes of Nature, the character of the experiment varying with the stage of the pupil's knowledge.

Attempts are being made to teach geography by moving-pictures, but here again the same defects appear. Most of the so-called geographical films are merely the " Travel Subjects " of the picture palace,—another attempt to make a subject fit both the theatre and the schoolroom. Such films are useless except to form a pictorial interlude in text-book explanation. Yet there is a remarkable scope for geographical films. Let

(5) Exhausted by its Struggles the Chick rests in
the Sun.

(6) A few Hours later the Chick takes to the Water.

The " Birth of a Moor-hen." A wonderful series of moving-
pictures taken by an amateur lady cinematographer.

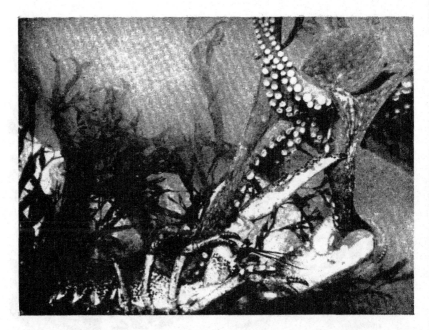

FIGHT BETWEEN A LOBSTER AND AN OCTOPUS.

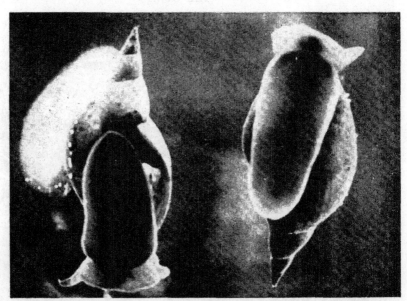

THE STORY OF THE WATER-SNAIL.

it be assumed that the lesson is about the birth of a river. The teacher dwells at length upon the possible sources, upon the tributaries that increase the volume of water during its journey, upon the navigable reaches and the traffic, and lastly upon the discharge of the waters into the ocean.

Cinematographically the rise and growth of the river may be shown far more graphically and attractively. The pupil can see every phase. The source may be an insignificant spring, the outflow from a lake, or the melting ice of a glacier. Its rapid growth can be depicted by showing the inflow of its tributaries and the many sudden changes through which it passes, its rapids and its falls, while the fact that water follows the path of least resistance may be illustrated by showing the evidences of erosion and the manner in which the river has cut its channel through friable soil, or taken advantage of a breach in a rocky rampart. At the same time the pupil can be introduced to the utility of the waterway, especially upon its upper reaches, by pictures of the craft found thereon and the traffic in which they are engaged. The varying force of the current can be illustrated, and also the flotsam and jetsam that has been brought down. Finally, gaining the lower reaches, steam and motor navigation begins, with towns and cities on the banks, and in conclusion the pupil may be given an idea of the immensity of the estuary together with the life and industry at this point. In addition some impression of the delta can be conveyed with moving-pictures of the way in which the detritus brought down from the upper reaches, is deposited at the mouth, forming islands and sand-banks, clothed with vegetation, and, if not developed, inhabited by wild fowl.

The preparation of such a film is certain to occupy a long time, and is somewhat expensive, but these items must be disregarded if the school-room is to have what it requires. A film of this character would have to be divided into certain lengths, each of which would correspond with a lesson, for the subject is too vast to be assimilated in a few minutes. Cramming by the aid of moving-pictures would be worse than under present conditions. In many cases the camera will show that existing text-book teachings are erroneous or need modification. Some idea of the utility of the cinematograph in this one particular field has been revealed by the films of the Shackleton and Scott Antarctic expeditions. They have brought home more vividly than anything else the meaning of the eternal snow, ice and cold, associated with the Polar regions, and they have served to dispel many false ideas.

So far the greatest success achieved by the

motion-pictures in the field of education is in connection with natural history. Many wonderful films bearing upon animal life have been prepared and have created sensations. The text-books tell much about the life and habits of the various members of the animal kingdom, but in this case the text-book often happens to be wrong. Mr. Frank A. Newman, an industrious animal photographer, devoted months to the preparation of a film 5,500 feet in length dealing with certain phases of animal life. He confined his efforts to the study of those creatures which are familiar to all. Incidentally, he proved the value that a highly instructive film possesses in the market, for within sixty days of its first appearance upon the screen, over £8,000 or $40,000 was realised from the disposal of the rights to exploit the film in different countries.

Pictures dealing with animal, bird, fish or reptile life never fail to command high prices. Indescribable patience is demanded in their preparation. Months may pass and yield only a few hundred feet of suitable material, and the photographer has to resort to the most extraordinary devices to take the subjects in their natural environment. One worker, who set himself the task of filming the kingfisher, discovered the haunts of his quarry, and then quietly commenced to establish himself in its vicinity. He had to be exceedingly cunning in his movements, masking the position he had assumed in four feet of water, with a clump of tree boughs. Concealed in this ambuscade he approached the bird, moving with extreme care, so as to convey the impression that the boughs were drifting with the stream. Behind this ambush he placed his camera, clamping it to a heavy floating base, which was anchored. In this way he was able to move undetected. When he thought that the time had come for an exposure, he commenced to turn the handle, but the whirr of the mechanism scared the bird, and he was forced to wait some time, until its courage revived and it came back. He then mounted a second camera on the floating base, and this, being empty of film, was set in motion every time the bird returned, until it grew accustomed to the unusual noise. After a few days the bird took no further notice of the sound, and then the pictures could be taken with comparative ease. Altogether some seven weeks were occupied in obtaining about 200 feet of film, during which time the operator had often to stand for hours at a time in four feet of water, awaiting his opportunities. How completely his strategy and patience were rewarded may be gathered from the fact that in one incident, where the bird is shown devouring a fish it has caught, it perched upon a branch of

THE HEAD OF THE TORTOISE.

THE HAWK MOTH.

SNAKE SHEDDING ITS SKIN OR "SLOUGH."

From the " Cinema College," by permission of the   *Motograph Co.*

THE SNAKE AND ITS SHED SLOUGH.

the ambuscade, barely four feet from the lens, completely unaware of the fact that its actions were being recorded.

Another indefatigable worker is Mr. J. C. Bee Mason, whose speciality is the filming of insect life. He has produced four films depicting the honey bee. As studies they are intensely interesting, and they bring out the characteristics of the subject in a most attractive manner. The average worker might hesitate to film such a subject at close quarters. The bee is very quick to resent intrusion and disturbance in a way peculiarily its own. Mr. Mason himself admits that in the early days he received very severe punishment, but he stuck to his camera and his work with the result that in the course of time he became accustomed to the attacks of the bees and to-day a sting has no more effect upon him than upon a deal board. The result of this patience is reflected in the excellence of his films which bring bee life most intimately before the spectator. The bee is always an object of interest, and in this particular case his films have brought Mr. Mason over £2,000, or $10,000.

Although here and there one comes upon a film which exactly meets with the requirements of the schoolroom, the majority can make no such claim. They are merely instructive, in an amusing kind of way, and in the picture palace they come as a welcome relief from transpontine drama and buffoonery. Fortunately, at the present moment, there is a growing tendency to make films which the schools will really welcome. One concern is studying the situation very closely. This is the Motograph Film Company of London, which has completed contracts with the most prominent European scientific cinematographers for their entire output of educational, scientific and natural history subjects. It is also endeavouring to persuade the eminent teachers of certain subjects to commit their work to the celluloid film instead of to printed books. It is a difficult quest because the professors are apt to regard the cinematograph as a joke. At the same time, once the development becomes started upon the correct lines, it cannot fail to meet with success.

The independent worker also is being encouraged by the Motograph Film Company, and the cinematographic student of scientific subjects has a very profitable market open to him. The prices paid for the films naturally vary according to their merit, but this company is prepared to pay from 2s. 6d. to 21s.—from 60 cents to $5—per foot of film for subjects which meet with its approval. The lengths may range from 50 to 6,000 feet. Recently, an independent lady worker, who in her spare time had given attention to filming the "Life of a Moorhen," showing the building of the nest, laying of the eggs, hatching and rearing of the young, sub-mitted her film to this concern. Some two-and-a-half years had been expended upon this subject, but the quality and the incidents depicted were so excellent that the 1,000 feet of film was bought for £650 ($3,250). This film has proved that the highest class of work must be obtained from the independent worker, or amateur, if that word is preferred, for the simple reason that time is no object, the task is not hurried, and no effort is spared to obtain the finest results. Another instructive film bought by this concern shows "Big Game Hunting in the North Pole Icefields." It intro-duces one to the polar bear. Altogether this subject extends over 8,000 feet, but for a selected length of 1,900 feet the sum of £2,000 ($10,000) was paid. In the case of another celebrated Arctic film, taken during the two years' imprison-ment of the Whitney expedition in the frozen zone, and about 6,000 feet in length, the same company gave £3,000 ($15,000) for the English rights alone.

Although the cinematograph has failed to make a very pronounced advance among our educational institutions, it has proved a striking success in education of another kind. This is in regard to the propaganda for improving health and hygiene. This movement has reached its highest stage of development in the United States. The "Swat the Fly" movement, which declared a relentless war against the common house-fly, was powerfully assisted by the exhibition of films depicting the fly at work in the dissemination of disease. Free exhibitions have been given throughout the United States for the purpose of bringing home to the public the serious menace that this insect offers to the welfare of the community. One or two of the films used for the purpose were bought from England, where they had been used in the picture palaces. But the organisation pledged to the extermination of the fly turned them to a far more serious purpose, and its work has met with remarkable success.

Another series of health films bear upon the "Great White Scourge." They are being exhibited freely and are bringing home to the public the terrible ravages wrought by tuberculosis. The dreaded bacillus is shown at its fell work, and the different stages of the disease are pictorially represented. Then follow a series of photographs showing how it is transmitted, and lastly some pictorial suggestions as to how it may be combated, at least in its early stages, by fresh air and sanatorium treatment.

The success of the fly and White Scourge campaigns has resulted in the preparation of other films dealing with the public health, while many local authorities have taken up the idea for the purpose of improving the conditions of their localities. Many of the films used for the purpose are prepared by amateur workers, especially when the subject is of local importance, and their ventures are proving highly profitable. Experience has proved in no uncertain manner that moving-pictures will soon be the world's most powerful educator.

CHAPTER XVIII

PHOTO-PLAYS AND HOW TO WRITE THEM

THE vogue of the picture palace has created a new profession. This is the writing of plays especially for cinematographic production. In the early days the handful of producers engaged in the craft had no difficulties in meeting their needs in this direction. The producer conceived and worked out his own ideas. The market was small, the output was restricted, and it did not matter whether the plots were good, bad, or indifferent. The public was quite content with the dramatic fare supplied upon the screen, being more impressed by the novelty of the performance than by its merits.

But with the rage for picture palaces the whole business underwent a transformation. The public, having outlived the era of curiosity, and having shown by its patronage that it regarded the picture palace in the same light as a theatre or music hall, grew more and more critical. It demanded stronger plots, improved mounting and acting, as well as better photographic quality. As new firms entered the producing field, competition became acute, and the whole photo-play industry automatically transferred itself from the pioneer to the accomplished master of stage-craft. The producer, unable to prepare his scenarios himself, sought the assistance of the amateur playwright, just as the editor of a periodical solicits contributions to fill his pages.

It was a golden opportunity for the unknown struggling dramatist. Foiled hitherto by lack of chance, the power of the privileged few, and the absence of enterprise displayed by theatrical managers, he handed his work to the upstart rival, the picture-play producer. It was a wise move. The dramatist did not, indeed, secure that measure of publicity upon the screen which might have been his lot upon the boards, but the financial returns were more regular. As he developed his inclinations, and his work became appreciated, he was able to anticipate a comfortable income, owing to the steady demand that arose for his handiwork. To-day the embryo dramatist never bestows a thought upon writing for the stage; the cinematograph will absorb all that he can produce, and as rapidly as he can complete it.

No longer need a budding genius starve unknown and unappreciated in a garret. If his work possesses any merit the cinematograph will turn it to profitable account. About three hundred picture-plays are placed upon the world's market every week, and consequently the consumption of plots is enormous. What is more important from the author's point of view is the expanding nature of this market, where supply cannot keep pace with demand, and the proportionate improvement that is manifest in the scale of remuneration. Ten years ago a plot seldom fetched more than five shillings or a dollar; to-day the same material will command anything between £5 and £50—$25 to $250. In this field of activity reputation counts for nothing. The play and the play only is the thing. The picture palace is the poor man's theatre, and this class of play-goer is relentlessly emphatic in condemnation, and equally enthusiastic in praise. It appreciates novelty in plot, and that is the one point the author has to bear in mind. So it is clear that the unknown playwright has everything in his favour; in fact, his work is generally preferred to that of the skilled writer. It contains the very best efforts of its creator; the other is probably of poor quality, because the man with a name does not realise what the people want, and thinks that for the cinematograph anything is good enough.

The desire of the photo-play producer to encourage unknown writers has led to the inevitable result. He is inundated with plots and

By permission of the

Motograph Co.

EXTERIOR VIEW OF THE DUMMY COW USED BY MESSRS. NEWMAN FOR TAKING MOVING-PICTURES OF WILD ANIMALS, SHOWING DOOR AT SIDE.

By permission of the   *Motograph Co.*

MR. FRANK NEWMAN AND HIS CAMERA HIDDEN WITHIN A
HOLLOW TREE TRUNK.

The utmost concealment is necessary to secure wild-life
under natural conditions.

suggestions of every description, written by every type of man, woman, and child. Needless to say, a large proportion of the submitted contributions are wildly impossible, or contain plots which have been worn so thread-bare that there is no possible chance of dressing them in a new guise. Fortunately the task of sifting the wheat from the chaff is not exacting. A hurried scan of the opening lines generally suffices to show whether the subject is excellent, passable, or hopeless.

Picture-play writing is an art, science, or whatever one likes to call it, which can be cultivated. The average person, at some time or other, is sure to have an idea—it may be an idle fleeting thought—which is capable of being turned to useful account. The picture-play producer knows this very well, and accordingly holds out every inducement in the hope that sooner or later he may light upon something brilliant. A suggestion need only have some small germ of possibility, but the producer, from his experience of the theatre, and of the requirements of the picture palace, can take that germ and evolve it in the most effective manner.

Under these circumstances the question arises "How should a photo-play be prepared ?" While there is no golden rule, and while each producer works in his own way, it is possible to give a few hints to the beginner. A glance at the manuscript is enough to inform the reader whether the author is a raw hand at the work or otherwise, and although every manuscript is reviewed, more interested attention is attracted by a contribution which is set out upon more or less methodical lines.

In the first place it is just as well to remember that the photo-play producer of to-day is a man of wide experience. In most cases he has graduated upon the stage, and has probably passed through all the phases between a touring company and a well-known theatre. As a result of this drilling he will have assumed a wide perspective. Sheer ability will have brought him to the control of the cinema-studio stage, where the work is most exacting, and where there is a very great demand for ingenuity and resource. Having mastered the intricacies and possibilities of the photo-play stage, and what can be done by photography, he will be a thorough master of craft. The greater number of the play-producers retained by the foremost firms are men who climbed to the top rung in the theatrical profession and merely went over to the motion-picture studio because it offered them greater scope for their prowess and knowledge. Indeed, one might go so far as to say that, unless a man has served his apprenticeship behind the footlights, he is an indifferent play-producer, because he will be ignorant of stage-craft and the technique of the profession.

A man of such experience and ability is able to sum up the value of a plot in an instant. Consequently the author is well advised to condense his plot into as few words as possible— the briefer the outline the better. In some instances it is not even necessary to indicate the characters, the period, or the scene. The plot is the only thing that is wanted: the producer, as he reads it, will conjure up in his mind the period, environment, atmosphere, and characters, wherewith such and such a story may best be worked out.

There is one well-known Continental producer who never asks for more than a bald statement of the plot. If it can be conveyed in six lines he is more than satisfied. On one occasion, while seated at lunch, one of the party jestingly suggested an idea. Without a word of comment the producer scribbled the suggestion upon the back of an envelope. Returning to the studio an hour or so later, he handed a note to one of his staff, indicated how he would like it worked out, the colleague fitted in the characters, evolved the scenes, period, and situations, and the next morning the play was staged.

One of the foremost French picture-play

producers follows a similar practice. He has a staff of eight writers whose sole duty is the preparation of scenarios for production. Plots as they flit through the minds of these men are jotted down and pigeon-holed. The outside contributions which come in with every post are scanned, and those thought suitable are dissected, their ideas are torn out and re-committed to paper, for filing, while the author is rewarded with payment according to the merit of his work. At this establishment no lengthy scenario submitted by an unknown writer is considered. Time is too valuable when eight or ten stages have to be kept going. The staff is fully occupied upon the work in hand, and cannot wade through pages of often indecipherable hand-writing. The method of this particular producer in the case of an ordinary play is to have an abstract, prepared by the retained scenario writer, indicating the scenes, their sequence, characters, and other details, with a brief synopsis of the plot, the whole being set out upon a sheet of foolscap. Upon this material the producer works, explaining to the company the story of the play and the situations, as they progress step by step.

Many producers, however, prefer the scenario to be submitted in a more complete form, though requirements of brevity and terseness must be observed. They like the list of characters to be given, together with a suggested period and setting. The cast should be kept as small as possible, as a plethora of characters in a photoplay is apt to be bewildering. Also the producer can amplify the cast if he wishes to do so. The plot should be set out in narrative form. A bald synopsis is quite sufficient because the scenario expert will judge the merits of the manuscript from this alone. In order to assist the producer the main points and situations may be indicated. After the synopsis there should be some suggestions for working out the story scene by scene. These are not essential, but they sometimes give the reader a better impression of the story, and help him in staging the play. The chances are a hundred to one that the play never will be staged as written by the author, yet its brief evolution is often appreciated.

When the author works out his plots he must steer clear of introducing wild impossibilities or hopelessly impracticable suggestions. The producer is admittedly a clever man, and is able to get wonderful effects with the aid of the camera, nor does he hesitate to employ trickery when it will further his purpose, but there are limitations even to trick photography. There was one manuscript in which the author, after taking his villain through adventures innumerable, suggested a sensational means of eliminating him altogether. The man was speeding across a frozen river to escape the vengeance of the hero when the ice opened up suddenly, let him through, and then closed on him to hide him from sight and memory. Needless to say, this plot met with scanty consideration. In another case the plot turned upon a lady's ring. The lady was standing by a river, and the ring slipped from her finger into the water to be caught and swallowed by a fish. Some days later the hero was fishing in the same stream. He had a bite, hooked his catch, cut it open, and found the ring. It is difficult to say who experienced the most amazement, the hero when he opened his fish, or the producer when he read the story.

In the photo-play profession it is novelty of the plot which brings success. The farther the author can get away from conventionality, the bigger will be the reward. This is where the average amateur shows deficiency. He is content to follow the footsteps of others. Again, many photo-play writers, instead of striving to be original, prefer to steal ideas from a novelist or short story writer. This work, needless to say, is sheer waste of time. The producer and his staff follow the periodicals and the publishing seasons very closely, so that it is easy for them to detect a stolen plot. Moreover, it must be remembered that to-day the leading producing firms have arrangements with authors, publishers and editors, for the exclusive use of their productions. These sources form a stand-by, as it were, to be brought into use when the fount of original scenarios dries up. When novels and magazine stories are to provide fare for the screen the producer entrusts the work of adaptation to one of his staff who has a more intimate idea of what is required, and will perform the task far more satisfactorily than the ordinary contributor.

The photo-play author has one great advantage over his colleague who writes for the stage. The latter has to supply dialogue, and often the success or failure of his work turns upon this factor. In writing for the screen dialogue is a lost quantity. It is action which is required, because the spectator has to follow the play from what he sees, and not from what he hears. Accordingly the requirements of action must be kept in mind. In the average studio the actor either extemporises dialogue to fit the part or situation, or else the producer prompts him.

It is true that one or two producers stipulate that the photo-play shall be written out in detail as if it were to be played behind the footlights, but such producers may be set down as incompetent or behind the times. A few years ago one of the Continental firms insisted that every play should be written out in full, but a few months' experience showed the folly of this procedure. Plays mounted in this manner lacked that grip and movement which is necessary in photographic pantomime. The audience could not retain the thread of the story, and the interest consequently flagged. The members of the company, being compelled to learn their lines, and to rehearse continually, went through their parts like puppets. Accordingly this method of mounting and acting has been abandoned in favour of the other in which the company, absolutely ignorant of the plot and story, is taken through it step by step and maintained at concert pitch throughout.

The writer should make a point of selecting a striking or catchy title for his work. Often when the plot itself is useless the producer will buy the manuscript merely to apply the title to some other production.

A word of warning may be given to the inexperienced photo-play author. Advertisements are freely inserted in the various periodicals offering to teach the art of writing plays for the cinematograph, and to submit the plots to the various producers in the manner of a literary agency. No matter how speciously and attractively the advertisements are written, the offers they contain should not be accepted. The author will do best to submit his work directly to the producer and to treat with him alone. The art cannot be taught by schools ; it can only be acquired by experience. Nor does the agency possess more favourable opportunities for getting the work accepted than the writer himself, while the so-called expert who maintains that he can lick a plot into shape is merely a charlatan. If the plot is good, whether written by a raw or a highly trained hand, it will command its price, because the producer is no respecter of persons. Also, by treating directly, the author comes into touch with the producer, and often learns points and receives encouragement which cannot be transmitted through a middle man.

How is the work rewarded ? This is a question which is often asked. So far as the British market is concerned the photo-play author receives scant encouragement. British enterprise has not risen to the level of that of the United States or the Continent. The British firms neither realise the value of a good plot nor the advantages of prompt and smart business methods. Here and there may be found a firm which is keenly alive to the value of the outside worker, but they are few and far between. On the other hand the American and Continental houses give an immediate decision, treat the outside contributor kindly, extend profitable words of advice if the work is promising, and pay promptly. A plot for which a British firm considers 10s. 0d. ($2.50) to be an adequate remuneration will realise $25 (£5) in the American market. The British producer will consider £1 ($5) to be a princely price for a good plot, and so long as this impression is retained the British photo-plays will remain inferior to their competitors. On the other hand, the American firms deal liberally with their authors, and are quite prepared to pay from $25 to $150—£5 to £30. Fortunately signs of awakening are becoming evident among the British firms. Good plots, like gold nuggets, are somewhat scarce, and one or two of the latest and most progressive establishments now pay up to £10 ($50).

Picture-play producers are finding greater and greater difficulty in obtaining first-class plots. The standard of excellence has been set so high, owing to the extremely critical character of the picture palace patron, that the highest work only now stands a chance of being accepted. The rivalry among the producers has become keen, because a strong picture-play can command a world-wide sale. One Italian firm, in the effort to forge ahead of its competitors, went so far as to offer a prize of £1,000 ($5,000) for the best scenario in open competition. It is admitted among the manufacturers that within the course of the next few years the royalty system must come into operation, so that the photo-play author will be elevated to the level of his confrère writing for the theatre.

In France a society has been founded for the protection of photo-play writers. This organisation protects its members by securing higher rates of payment, by introducing the work of beginners to the film-producers, and last, but not least, by advertising the writer.

Ten years ago the picture-play author was regarded with disdain, and was considered to be little more than an indifferent literary hack. To-day he is regarded as a powerful force. From the lowest and most ill-paid level he is rising to the highest rungs, where his rewards are excellent and his opportunities unbounded.

CHAPTER XIX

RECENT DEVELOPMENTS IN STAGE PRODUCTIONS

ALTHOUGH the mounting and staging of photo-plays has been greatly improved, the art has still many imperfections. This is partly due to the conservative character of the industry. There is a lack of initiative and enterprise; the producers are content to keep in the one groove which was established years ago. No one can deny that enormous sums of money are expended upon the mounting of the productions, nor assail them from the photographic viewpoint. But there is a lack of art which at times is sadly jarring.

This was to be expected. When the English pioneers embarked upon the play-producing business they knew nothing about stage-craft. Their ambition was rather to perfect the photographic quality of the films. So rapidly did the movement advance, however, and so insistent was the public in its demands for better, larger, and more lavishly staged plays, that the pioneer found himself out-distanced. At this juncture came the man who had won his spurs in the theatre, and who was thoroughly expert in the technique of stage-craft. His professional knowledge lifted the art out of the hands of the pioneers, who retired from the scene.

The introduction of the professional element commenced in France, and was taken up immediately by the Americans. These two countries went ahead so rapidly that Great Britain was soon left behind. The world became flooded with French and American productions, and in this healthy race the latter soon went ahead and took premier position. The French industry, being threatened, pulled itself together, and taking a cue from American methods it overhauled its organisations and increased its expenditure, with the result that it soon attained the level of excellence achieved by the United States. At a later date the Italian industry, which was in a languishing condition, followed suit. Money was sunk in the enterprise, huge studios were built, and talented artists were engaged to act before the moving-picture camera.

Great Britain lagged in this race, and it is only recently that the British producers, by a change of method have been able to make up the leeway. The British movement was rather of a sporadic nature. It was left to one or two enterprising firms to show the way. But others have followed, and to-day there is the keenest rivalry in producing, nor is expense considered so long as the public gets what it wants. To sink £3,000 ($15,000) in a single production has become quite a common venture.

In many cases, however, in spite of these changes, photo-plays still follow the lines that prevailed ten years ago. The blemishes, defects, and anachronisms are just as pronounced now as they were then, though they are suffered in silence by the public. Many faults are hidden by the gorgeous and lavish mounting of the scenes, while the rapid action of the players serves to distract attention from the shortcomings of the environment. But the feeling of actuality, which ought to be the great feature of the cinematograph, is missing. The scenic accessories might be left out for all the effect that they produce.

As a matter of fact the photo-play stage occupies to-day the position of the theatre twenty years ago. The scenery is for the most part make-shift, crudely painted in the neutral black and white, the stock room being ransacked to discover pieces of canvas to fit the situation. There is no attempt to create an artistic effect. Also there is an entire absence of reality or individuality. A cell scene, for instance, bears every sign of being built of canvas and battens, and so does the exterior of a mediæval castle,

From the *"Cinema College,"* by permission of the

Motograph Co.

Tree Lizard, with a Spider, which it has Captured, in its Mouth.

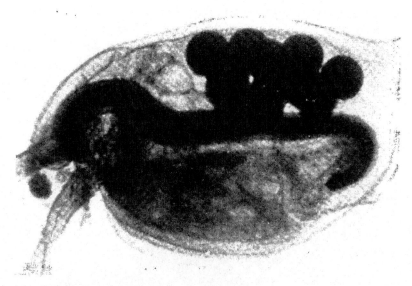

THE DIGESTIVE ORGANS AND EGGS OF A WATER FLEA.

THE MOVING-PICTURE NATURALIST AND THE LIZARD AT HOME.

or the inside of a conservatory, and completed by a factory hand.

Sometimes the shortcomings of the studio-stage are avoided by setting the plays in an outdoor surrounding, and in this instance a far more realistic effect is produced. The audience is unconsciously carried away. This has been specially realised by some of the American, Danish and Italian firms.

In France the Gaumont Company has shown equal enterprise. So far as possible the elaborate productions of this company are acted in a scene suited to the plot, whether it be a sixteenth century castle or a modern hotel. There is ample opportunity for doing this, and the present popularity of the photo-play proves the wisdom of the policy. During the summer months as many as six different companies will be working in as many different corners of Europe, acting plays in the open air for the picture palaces. Even the interiors in Gaumont films are often real and not merely constructed for the occasion. As a rule the studio is used only during the winter when the climatic conditions are unfavourable for outdoor work. This is the chief reason why the Gaumont films to-day are in such demand, and why the company has forced its way to the front.

The conveyance of players to a suitable natural

setting is expensive, but it represents all the difference between success and failure. Of course, there are occasions when a natural setting demands a certain amount of artificial embellishment. This was the case in the filming of Hamlet, as presented by Sir Forbes Robertson and his company. A sea background and a battlemented castle were required. The former was quite easy to find, but the combination of the two was more difficult. The problem was solved by the choice of Lulworth Cove as the scene and by erecting a solid set to represent the castle. In this case the preparation of the extemporised castle was so thorough and careful that it looks like a weather-beaten stone building.

The photo-play stage will be forced to emulate the current practice of the theatre. It must bring the artist to bear upon the work. At the moment it is merely a combination of the photographer and the stage-manager or producer. The latter is not always an artist, though he is clever at making existing facilities suit his purpose. The theatre is holding its own principally because it respects the artistic side of the issue. Individuality is encouraged. The photo-play stage will have to follow the same line of action. Directly this is done the picture palace will become a spirited rival of the theatre.

For this reason the efforts of Sir Hubert von Herkomer, the eminent British artist, are being followed with interest. He was attracted to the photo-play producing business owing to the artistic atrocities perpetrated by the professional producer of film plays. He is not attempting to achieve any revolution, except in the mounting and acting of plays for the camera, but in this sphere he hopes to bring about a recognition of the part that the artist must play.

There is a complete absence of sensationalism about the artist-producer's work, and in this respect he goes against the conventions. He is deliberately flouting many of the accepted tenets of the photo-play production, and his attitude is certain to meet with some hostile criticism. But from the realist point of view he is correct. His matter-of-fact productions give verisimilitude to the scene and story, and brings them within the range of probability. There is no straining after effect. No detail is introduced unless it has a distinct bearing on the subject. The costumes are faithful to the last button. If a sixteenth century farmhouse is wanted, it is built, and built so well that in the picture it has every appearance of having been built of stone.

A feature which will be appreciated in the Herkomer productions is the suppression of the harsh and distressing blacks, greys and whites,

244 PRACTICAL CINEMATOGRAPHY

which under brilliant illumination often convey the impression of snow. Nor do the players seem to be suffering from anæmia. These appear to be trivial matters in themselves, but they greatly affect the ultimate whole. The robust aspect of the peasant who lives out of doors is faithfully conveyed, and he is thrown up in sharp contrast to the white-faced townsman. In the conventional picture-play, on the other hand, there is no individuality of facial expression, because one and all are made up in the same way.

Sir Hubert von Herkomer has commenced his work in a logical way. He confesses that until he began it he knew nothing about it. He was not harassed by a partial knowledge of how things are done. He is essentially a pioneer, content to work out his own ideas, and possessed of views upon stage-craft which are not to be despised. They had a good effect upon the theatre twenty or thirty years ago, and have lately been revived by another enthusiast. So Sir Hubert von Herkomer is not likely to be the slave of tradition.

He maintains that in the average photo-play everything is sacrificed to rapid action. This is true, and it is done purposely to distract attention from the weakness of the rest. The spectator must fix his attention upon the characters or he loses the thread of the story. No time is given him to see the deficiency of atmosphere or environment. The result is that everything is rushed through as if the villain and hero were racing the clock. To realise this it is only necessary to follow the film-play of a well-known historical story. Familiarity with the incident here gives the spectator a chance of taking in the setting and the mounting. If there are mistakes, interest gives way to mirth and all concentration is lost. The picture is followed with no more enthusiasm than a pantomime. This is the main reason why producers are chary of portraying well-known historical episodes upon the screen. One educational authority has described such films as burlesques, and that is among the causes of opposition to the cinematograph as an educational medium. In one instance an attempt was made to film an incident in one of Fenimore Cooper's stories with white actors made up as Red Indians. It was acted in a well-kept private forest instead of in the wild woods of Canada. But young and old proved to be too familiar with this author's works. They had too true a notion of the Canadian timber wilderness to be impressed by the substitute on the screen, and received the presentation with the ridicule it deserved. The sight of a Red Man slouching through the bush with out-turned feet and trying to conceal himself behind a tree less than six inches in thickness, proved to be merely comic. But other things equally ridiculous are found in many of the films of to-day, and that is the reason why the scenes are so judiciously rushed.

By slowing down the speed of acting, though without reducing the sustained interest, Sir Hubert von Herkomer contends that the public will be put in a position to grasp the whole subject, and will be able to follow it more rationally and comprehensibly. At the same time the players will have time and scope to perform their parts properly. There is not the least reason why this should not be achieved without allowing the action to flag or the interest to drop.

The lighting of the subject is another important feature to which Sir Hubert von Herkomer is giving attention. The illumination must be arranged to suit the situation, and as cine-matography offers the utmost latitude in this respect, it is unnecessary to rush to violent extremes. In many productions the studio stage is suffused with such an intense glare that all facial expression and shadows are sacrificed. Sir Hubert has realised how great is the scope for improvement in this direction, and is altering the whole principle of stage lighting. Similarly, in outdoor work he is supplementing sunshine with arc lights, so as to secure the steady illumination necessary for good effects. The combination of brilliant daylight and artificial illumination is a novelty in photo-play production, but when the action is taking place under trees, where the shadows are heavy and in sharp contrast with scattered patches of brilliant sunlight, the players are apt to present a phantom appearance. Sometimes they are scarcely distinguishable. The introduction of auxiliary light relieves the shadowy places and softens the general effect. Needless to say the manipulation of powerful arc lights under such conditions demands skilful handling, but in the Herkomer films the improved results certainly show that the labour is not wasted.

Whether the combination of artist and producer will prove successful time alone can show. There will be a certain amount of commercial opposition, lacking in artistic feeling, and hostile to innovation. But the appearance of the artist and his resolution to work out his schemes logically should surely be encouraged by the public. The same reforms that changed and improved the theatre, enabling it to hold its own against the all-conquering picture palace, have a mission to the latter also. They can lift it to the higher level that is its obvious destiny.

CHAPTER XX

CONSIDERING the position which the motion-picture has attained in our social and industrial life, the establishment of national cinematograph laboratories appears not only to be opportune, but necessary. At the present moment, if one conceives an idea for the solving of some abstruse problem by means of animated photography, one is handicapped by the lack of opportunity and facilities for carrying out the work. Either the apparatus required must be made specially, or purchased, in which case heavy expenditure may be incurred, or, one must go to Paris and make use of the Marey Institute, either by becoming a member of it or by serving as the representative of a contributory society. There, one is able to pursue the line of study quietly, easily, and economically, and, even if the ultimate results are disappointing, or the cherished theories prove to be untenable, certain benefits are sure to accrue from the experiments. The time is not wasted.

The Marey Institute is unique and wonderful. Its operations are world-wide. Its founder,

Dr. E. J. Marey, was a prodigious worker who pursued his scientific investigations without any idea of personal gain. When first he entered the arena of science he began his experiments in a large room upon the fifth floor of a house in the Rue de l'ancienne Comédie, Paris, which formerly belonged to the Comédie Française. Here he fitted up as good a laboratory as he could afford, dividing the spacious apartment, by wooden partitions, into working and living rooms. His studies soon aroused widespread attention, and their results were subsequently embodied in his classical work, " The Graphic Method." But some ten years before this volume appeared his investigations had received recognition. In 1867 the Minister of Public Instruction offered him the use of a laboratory at the College of France, so as to be able to carry out his researches to better advantage.

During this period he invented numerous instruments — the sphymograph, cardiograph, pneumograph, thermograph, and odograph—with which he made invaluable contributions to scientific knowledge. It was Konig's work which attracted Marey to animated photography, as a handmaid of science, the outcome being his greatest discovery, which he named chrono-photography. Marey was much impressed by Jannsen's astronomical revolver with which, in

1873, a series of photographs of the transit of Venus were taken in 70 seconds. This caused him to build a photographic gun, with which gulls in flight were secured. The work of Muybridge, the English investigator residing in San Francisco, aroused his enthusiasm to the highest pitch, and enabled him to perfect his system of taking a series of successive photographs upon a single glass plate. Finally, in 1893, he produced his first moving-picture camera working with celluloid films.

But some twenty years before this last achievement he had conceived the idea for an International Institution where experiments of this character, in connection with motion photography, might be carried out to the advantage of the sciences. He realised that the elucidation of physiological phenomena was quite beyond the capacity of a single individual. He outlined his scheme at the Fourth Physiological Congress, held at Cambridge (England) in the early seventies, while Monsieur H. Kronecker, of Switzerland, a great admirer of Marey's work, who succeeded to the presidential chair of the Institution after the founder's death, urged a similar plea at an exhibition of scientific apparatus held in London in 1876.

Marey's broad-mindedness met with its reward. With the assistance of private friends and

By permission of the   *Motograph Co.*

A NOVEL "HIDE" CONTRIVED BY MR. J. T. NEWMAN WITH
CAMERA FIFTEEN FEET ABOVE THE GROUND.

The working platform is covered with boughs so as not to
alarm the forest life being cinematographed.

THE "HIDE" OPENED TO SHOW WORKING PLATFORM, TRESTLE
SUPPORT, OPERATOR AND CAMERA PLACED FIFTEEN FEET
ABOVE THE GROUND.

contemporary scientific societies throughout the world he obtained adequate funds for the establishment of the Institution, the necessity for which he had advanced so vigorously. The City of Paris gave valuable help by granting the use of a tract of land attached to its physiological station, and here Marey established a commodious building with spacious workrooms, a library, lecture hall, and other conveniences, for the profitable prosecution of cinematographic research.

Since the foundation of the " French Cradle of Cinematography," innumerable and valuable contributions to scientific knowledge have been made by investigators of all nationalities, who have gone to Paris to take advantage of the facilities offered. Many extraordinary films dealing with the various branches of science have been prepared. Many of the most prominent scientists of all nations, France, Great Britain, Germany, Italy, Roumania, Switzerland, the United States of America, arc numbered among its members.

It may be said truthfully that the Marey Institute has anticipated all the great developments that have been made during recent years concerning the instructional or informative side of film production. Unfortunately the original investigations were made so long ago, before the possibilities of animated photography were appreciated, that they have been forgotten by, or are unknown to, the present generation. Many an inventor, enthusiastic about a development which he has perfected in the art, has received a rude shock when his work became public and he learned that he had been forestalled years before at the Marey Institute.

Nearly all of the so-called scientific films, which arouse widespread interest to-day, were prepared originally at the Marey Institute. The combination of the cinematograph with the microscope, the X-rays, and other apparatus, the recording of the growth of plants and animals, the photographing of rapid movements all these were demonstrated at this establishment a generation ago.

Surely what has been possible at a French establishment is not beyond the resources of other countries? When one recalls the valuable assistance given to science by the French Institute, there should be no hesitation in other countries to emulate the idea, and to establish national institutions for a similar purpose. Animated photography is still in its infancy. Its educational and scientific possibilities are scarcely yet realised. There were many years during which no one realised the full advantages of ordinary photography in the provinces of investigation and experiment, and animated photography is passing through a similar phase. This is largely because of the showman, who is enterprising, and has captured the fort for himself. Probably no other industry has been responsible for the creation of so many million-aires in so short a period, yet there is no industry which can render so great a service to science.

It should not be difficult to establish national institutions, on Marey's lines, in every country which has great industrial and commercial interests at stake. So far as Great Britain is concerned it might be attached to the National Physical Laboratory at Teddington. This estab-lishment has an extensive array of scientific apparatus of all descriptions capable of being utilised in conjunction with the moving-picture camera, so that the additional outlay would not be excessive. Not only would it be possible to utilise the invention in connection with existing experiments, but independent and original investi-gation could be undertaken. There are many points of science which can be determined only by moving-pictures. Although Marey covered the ground very completely during his lifetime, as a perusal of "Movement" will show, many new spheres of application have appeared since his time. It is quite possible that if some of his investigations were repeated in the light of later knowledge, the new results would be quite as striking as the old.

In Germany the cinematographic laboratory might be attached to the world-famed testing laboratory at Charlottenburg. At present, although the recording instruments in use are of a most modern and perfect description, there are innumerable instances where improvement might be effected by photographic methods. The German military authorities were not slow to appreciate the value of Professor Cranz's system of photographing projectiles in flight. Directly the initial experiments were concluded the work was taken up by the War Department. Although certain particulars of the apparatus employed and its method of operation have been published, the essential details have been kept secret. It is admitted that the method evolved by Cranz is imperfect in certain features, but the authorities have the germ of a useful invention, and are now developing it independently. In Italy also the value of the cinematograph is being appreciated in a certain direction. The Minister of Marine has established a special department of photography and cinematography in Rome, after personal investigation of the utility of the invention during the naval manœuvres.

The United States of America has been no

more progressive than Great Britain in giving recognition to animated photography, but there are indications that this lethargic attitude is to be abandoned. Certain influential interests have suggested the establishment of a cinematographic bureau of standards, emphasising the usefulness of the invention for supplying measurements of time and work. Apart from this movement other independent enthusiasts have recommended the formation of moving-picture laboratories in connection with the various training institutions, so that students might be trained on the correct lines. Doubtless the perfection of continuous-record cinematography, and of cameras capable of working at the highest speeds, will stimulate the movement, for they provide a method of getting information which even the cinematograph has not hitherto been able to give.

There are a thousand problems incidental to industry and commerce which now defy solution, but could be solved by animated photography. Aviation, which at present is occupying the attention of every nation, is a case in point. The mechanical part of the science has been investigated minutely but little progress has been made in studying the effect of the air upon the planes, so as to discover the best forms of cutting edge. Present endeavour is content to work upon the results obtained by Marey with his chronophotographic apparatus some twenty years ago. No attempt has been made to ascertain whether it is possible to improve upon his work, or to determine whether the data he gathered is in need of modification. Another field of investigation is in regard to the testing of metals, woods, and other materials, to discover their behaviour under varying degrees of strain.

A national cinematographic laboratory need not be expensive either to establish nor to maintain. The Marey Institute might be taken as a model. After the death of Marey, in 1905, the means of carrying on the institution were completely reorganised. The work it was accomplishing was recognised as being too valuable to be allowed to cease. The French Government took up the question and decided to grant an annual subvention of £960 ($4,800). The German, Swiss, Russian, and other Governments, as well as various scientific institutions of all nations, also decided to subscribe regularly to its support. In this way, with the addition of some private subscriptions, about £1,500 ($7,500) is contributed annually. Other contributions are made in kind, such as the film, all of which is given by the firm of Lumière.

Considering the work accomplished by the Marey Institute it is maintained very economically. The annual expenses average about £1,200 or

$6,000. The paid staff comprises the assistant sub-director and an assistant, two highly skilled mechanics, and one or two minor officials, the important posts being filled honorarily.

Private investigators are encouraged to use the Institute and its equipment. The scientific institutions of the different countries are given certain facilities in return for a small payment. Thus an annual subscription of £40 ($200) entitles the representative of an institution to the widest use of the laboratory. He is not only given free and unrestricted use of all the apparatus, but is provided with a bedroom, so that his expenses are reduced to disbursements upon meals and other personal requirements. Everything requisite for his study, as well as accessories, such as light, film, developers, etc., are provided free of charge.

The laboratory is well provided with all sorts of appliances. There are cameras of various designs adapted to special classes of work, dark rooms for developing, rooms for experiments, a workshop with skilled mechanics, a library stocked with literature bearing upon cinematography and its relation to the sciences, and a large and lofty hall furnished with a projector and screen. As the Institute stands in its own grounds of over 3,000 square yards, there are ample facilities for out-door investigations.

The experimenter at this Institution has advantages placed at his disposal which will not be found elsewhere in any other part of the world. The majority of the appliances have been designed by the staff mechanics, and in their manufacture extreme ingenuity has been displayed. Much of the apparatus might possibly provide an income in the form of royalties if it were commercially exploited. But it is a rule of the Institute that no instrument may be patented. Its work is for the benefit of all.

Undoubtedly the near future will see the foundation of national cinematographic laboratories in some form or other. The value of animated photography is not yet appreciated. Directly the sciences realise its significance, and see that it constitutes an indispensable aid to investigation and research, the invention will be given the recognition it deserves. Then it will be turned into more useful channels than at present. Individual investigation will be encouraged, and discoveries more wonderful than any of which we know will be made.

INDEX

RADIO-CINEMATOGRAPHY, 147
—160
Rainey, Paul, 9
Rapid movement, record of,
108—116; projection of,
117—122
Records, continuous, 136;
apparatus, 137—138; scien-
tific experiments with, 139
—146
Reinforced screen, 158
Revolver, astronomical, 249—
250
Ries, Dr. J., investigations, 168
Robertson, Sir Forbes, in
picture play, 242
Ross lens, 23
Ruby light, the, 68

SCIENTIFIC investigation, 185
—196. *See also under* Experiments and investiga-
tions.
Slow movements, record and
projection of, 124—133
Soaking solution formula, 75
Speed, photographic and projecting, 16—20; slowing
down, 108—123; speeding
up, 124—134
Spitta, Dr., 164
Spoolwinder, 77

Sprocket, 28 (ill.)
Stock, 34
" String " galvanometer, 137
" Swat the Fly," health film,
222

THERMOGRAPH, the, 249.
Time registration, tuning-fork,
103—107; chronoscope, 111
—112
Trick films, difficulties of, 6
Tripod, 32—34
Tuning-fork control, 103—107

VIEW finder, the, 49

WILLIAMSON, Mr. James, 24;
micro - cinematographic
studies, 164
Williamson outfit, 10; camera,
8, 24 — 28 (ill.); printer,
80, 85—87 (ill.); focussing,
30, 38, 47; mounting, 31,
driving gear, 32; iris diaphragm, 43—46

X-RAYS and cinematography.
See Radio-cinematography.

ZEISS-TESSAR lens, 23—24, 43

BRADBURY, AGNEW, & CO. LD, PRINTERS, LONDON AND TONBRIDGE

0 1341 1660232 4

CPSIA information can be obtained
at www.ICGtesting.com
Printed in the USA
LVOW04s2107281116
514775LV00003BB/175/P

9 781363 438044